What is Qualitative Longitudinal Rese

## 'What is?' Research Methods series

Edited by Graham Crow

The 'What is?' series provides authoritative introductions to a range of research methods which are at the forefront of developments in the social sciences. Each volume sets out the key elements of the particular method and features examples of its application, offering a consistent structure across the whole series. Written in an accessible style by leading experts in the field, this series is an innovative pedagogical and research resource.

# What is

# qualitative longitudinal research?

Bren Neale

BLOOMSBURY ACADEMIC
LONDON • NEW YORK • OXFORD • NEW DELHI • SYDNEY

BLOOMSBURY ACADEMIC
Bloomsbury Publishing Plc
50 Bedford Square, London, WC1B 3DP, UK
1385 Broadway, New York, NY 10018, USA

BLOOMSBURY, BLOOMSBURY ACADEMIC and the Diana logo are trademarks
of Bloomsbury Publishing Plc

First published in Great Britain 2019

Cover design © Paul Burgess
Cover image © Eliks/Shutterstock

Bloomsbury Publishing Plc does not have any control over, or responsibility for, any
third-party websites referred to or in this book. All internet addresses given in this
book were correct at the time of going to press. The author and publisher regret any
inconvenience caused if addresses have changed or sites have ceased to exist, but
can accept no responsibility for any such changes.

A catalogue record for this book is available from the British Library.

A catalog record for this book is available from the Library of Congress.

ISBN: HB: 978-1-4725-2767-7
PB: 978-1-4725-3007-3
ePDF: 978-1-4725-2167-5
eBook: 978-1-4725-3081-3

Series: The 'What is?' Research Methods series

Typeset by Deanta Global Publishing Services, Chennai, India
Printed and bound in Great Britain

To find out more about our authors and books visit www.bloomsbury.com
and sign up for our newsletters.

*For my mother, Gwendoline*
*(1916–2017)*
*who lived through a century of change*

*and for my grandson, Luka*
*(b. 2017)*
*who will see the future unfold.*

# Contents

# Acknowledgements

This book is built on the accumulated wisdom of generations of researchers who have pioneered qualitative longitudinal research. It has been a privilege and pleasure to meet and work alongside a good number of these researchers in recent years. This was made possible through a series of research grants from the Economic and Social Research Council, including a mid-career fellowship, national and international seminar series, and funding for a five-year programme of qualitative longitudinal (QL) research and archiving (the *Timescapes Study*). I owe a particular debt of gratitude to my *Timescapes* colleagues, and to the affiliated researchers, archivists, secondary analysts and time theorists who enriched the programme. This was an exhilarating, cutting-edge environment to develop the ideas for this book. Many thanks also to Graham Crow, series editor, for the invitation to write this text, and for his support and encouragement, and Maria Giovanna Brauzzi and the team at Bloomsbury Academic for gently steering the project. Finally, special thanks (and apologies) to my family, especially to Alan, who read every word and was there every step of the way.

# Series editor's foreword

The idea behind this series is a simple one: to provide concise and accessible overviews of a range of frequently used research methods and of current issues in research methodology. Books in the series have been written by experts in their fields with a brief to write about their subject for a broad audience who are assumed to be interested but not necessarily to have any prior knowledge. The series is a natural development of presentations made in the 'What is?' strand at Economic and Social Research Council (ESRC) Research Methods Festivals which have proved popular both at the Festivals themselves and subsequently as a resource on the website of the ESRC National Centre for Research Methods.

Methodological innovation is the order of the day, and the 'What is?' format allows researchers who are new to a field to gain an insight into its key features, while also providing a useful update on recent developments for people who have had some prior acquaintance with it. All readers should find it helpful to be taken through the discussion of key terms, the history of how the method or methodological issue has developed and the assessment of the strengths and possible weaknesses of the approach through analysis of illustrative examples.

This thirteenth book in the series is devoted to QL research. In it, Bren Neale describes the growing interest that exists in the potential of a range of qualitative tools and techniques to capture how people's lives unfold over time. Appreciating the detail of individual journeys through the life course assists in understanding how trajectories are patterned as well as being remarkably diverse. Practitioners of QL research quickly become familiar with the conceptual, practical and ethical challenges of studying the unfolding character of people's routes through life. The meaning of time can be difficult to pin down, while the systematic study of processes over prolonged periods requires not only good organization and determination but also the ability to handle the presence of difficulties that inevitably feature in people's lives. To follow a life will be likely to involve encounters with sickness as well as health, privation as well as prosperity, and sorrow as well as happiness. But the rewards of following lives over time using qualitative methods are extensive, including the illumination of large-scale social change at a level that is more readily grasped than it is through the more abstract structural accounts that are associated with the analysis of quantitative data sets. It is for this reason that researchers are increasingly to be found exploring the complementarity of qualitative and quantitative longitudinal analysis, and Neale's contribution to this 'What Is?' series dovetails with that by Vernon Gayle and Paul Lambert. The two approaches may have different origins, but they do have several points of connection, not least the appreciation of how an event can take on the form of a turning point in a life story, and how such events are linked to broader patterns of social change.

The books in this series cannot provide information about their subject matter down to a fine level of detail, but they will equip readers with a powerful sense of reasons why it deserves to be taken seriously and, it is hoped, with the enthusiasm to put that knowledge into practice.

Graham Crow

# 1 Introducing qualitative longitudinal research

## Introduction

> At a time when social forces are making instability a way of life, researchers are developing new modes of enquiry that take account of the dynamic nature of people's lives. Approaches to 'thinking dynamically' have triggered the beginning of an intellectual revolution, one that blends insights from across the social sciences, merges quantitative and qualitative methodologies, combines macro and micro views of society and exploits the power of international comparison. (Leisering and Walker 1998, xiv)

Qualitative Longitudinal research (QL research, QLR or QPR) is a rich and evolving methodology for exploring the dynamic nature of people's lives. It has developed in piecemeal fashion across different research traditions, a process reflected in the varied labels used to describe it (from Longitudinal Ethnography to Qualitative Panel Studies). As the quotation above suggests, QL research is part of a broad 'temporal turn' in social enquiry that has emerged gradually over the past decades. With its dual identity (both longitudinal and qualitative), QL research spans two established methodological traditions. As a small but vital component of the longitudinal canon, it seeks to follow the same individuals or small collectives (households or varied forms of organization) prospectively, in 'real' time, as lives unfold. As part of the rich field of qualitative temporal studies, QL research explores dynamic processes through an in-depth, qualitative lens. This gives insights into how people narrate, understand and shape their unfolding lives and the evolving world of which they are a part. QL research is conducted *through* time; but it also engages with the temporal dimensions of experience, opening up the potential to 'think

1

dynamically' in creative, flexible and innovative ways. These features of QL research suggest it is part of a developing theoretical orientation, an emerging paradigm for social research that offers new and exciting ways to know and understand the social world.

## Thinking through time

The importance of time has long been recognized in social scientific research, but, as the introductory quotation shows, it has taken on new significance with the recognition of rapid social change in the contemporary world. Time is the lynchpin for understanding the essentially dynamic nature of lived experiences, and the relationship between personal lives and wider historical processes (Mills 1959). It is *through time* that we can begin to grasp the nature of social change and continuity, the mechanisms through which these processes unfold, and the ways in which structural forces shape the lives of individuals and groups and, in turn, are shaped by them. Indeed, it is *only* through time that can we can gain a better appreciation of how agency and structure, the micro and macro dimensions of experience, are interconnected and how they come to be transformed (Neale and Flowerdew 2003). In all forms of temporal research time is the driving force for research design and practice. It is the medium through which QL research is conducted. But it is also a rich theoretical construct and topic of enquiry that feeds into the generation and analysis of data.

One of the distinctive features of QL research is its capacity for a rich and flexible engagement with time. Yet this gives rise to a number of questions. How exactly do QL researchers engage with time? How does time as a social construct feed into research design, practice, ethics and analysis? Underpinning these questions is another: how is time itself conceptualized and understood? More broadly, what is the place of QL research within the established fields of temporal research that engage longitudinally and/or qualitatively with time? These basic questions about temporal theory, design and practice are explored and addressed in this volume.

## An evolving methodology

QL enquiry is rooted in a long-established tradition of qualitative temporal research that has evolved over the past century. What is relatively new, however, is the growing reflexivity of researchers as they have begun to delineate and document this approach and explore its theoretical underpinnings.[1] This, in turn, has fuelled a growing interest in and rapid uptake of QL research over the first two decades of the twenty-first century. Studies range from the lived experience of welfare reform and the dynamics of transport, to the temporalities of legal regulation and the delivery and impact of new health and social care interventions. Researchers from a wide range of disciplines in the arts, humanities and the social and natural sciences are routinely seeking to incorporate QL methods into their research designs. These developments have global reach and influence. Beyond the UK, studies are flourishing across Europe, Australia, Canada and the United States, and beginning to appear in sub-Saharan Africa. Funding has been provided by the UK central and devolved governments, British and international funding councils, independent research organizations such as the Joseph Rowntree Foundation, and global agencies such as the World Health Organization. In a parallel development, long-running TV documentaries that trace unfolding biographies, for example, the *Seven Up* series and *Child of our Time*, have popularized this approach and demonstrated its enduring appeal for global audiences.

Amid this rapid expansion, there have been calls for more guidance on the conduct of QL research and for some standardization of methodological techniques (Calman, Brunton and Molassiotis 2013). A narrowly prescriptive approach would clearly be counterproductive, given the exploratory, flexible, creative and porous nature of this methodology (Thomson and McLeod 2015). Nevertheless, crafting a QL study requires an adequate grounding in temporal theory, methods and ethics. This introductory text seeks to provide an overview of these features, from theoretical underpinnings to research practice.

Each chapter is designed to take the reader on a short research journey. In this introductory chapter, the historical development of QL enquiry is traced, and its place within the broad canon of temporal studies is explored. Chapter 2 ('Conceptual Foundations') takes the reader on a short journey through time. It considers how theoretical understandings of time can

---

[1] Edited collections within a burgeoning literature include Foster, Scudder, Colson and Kemper (1979), Huber and Van de Ven (1995), Kemper and Peterson Royce (2002), Thomson, Plumridge and Holland (2003), Millar (2007), Neale, Henwood and Holland (2012), Howell and Talle (2012), and Thomson and McLeod (2015). To date, Saldana (2003) stands out as a dedicated methods text.

be used to enrich empirical studies, and explores how the life course can be understood through varied temporal registers. Chapter 3 ('Crafting Qualitative Longitudinal Research') explores how time can be used empirically to build the longitudinal frame for a study, and to determine a sampling strategy. Chapter 4 ('Walking Alongside') considers the journeys that researchers take with their participants: how they are recruited into a study and their involvement sustained, and the ethical terrain within which these processes occur. Chapter 5 ('Journeys with Data') explores the rich range of tools and techniques used to generate and analyse temporal data. Throughout the text, readers are directed to key empirical sources and illustrative material that will help to flesh out the picture. A short concluding chapter ('Looking Back, Looking Forwards') sums up of the key themes of the book and assesses the strengths and challenges of QL enquiry. It also highlights a number of areas for future development (e.g. mixed longitudinal approaches, digital and arts-based methodologies and the reuse of existing data) that are touched upon only briefly in this volume.

## Mapping the field

The discussion below considers the place of QL methodology within the broad canon of temporal studies and traces its development over a century of scholarship. We start with longitudinal and life course research, and go on to consider a range of studies that make up the field of qualitative temporal research. In the process, the commonalities and differences between these varied approaches are explored and the distinctive features of QL research are illuminated. As the discussion below will show, the differences between these fields of enquiry are often a matter of disciplinary tradition rather than strict methodological divisions, giving scope for a productive blending of methods as these fields develop. Before mapping these fields, two basic dimensions of temporal engagement are introduced and clarified here. The ensuing discussion illustrates how these dimensions of time feed into research design.

## Engaging with time: Key dimensions

All temporal research constructs a moving picture of change and continuity in the social world. In each case a 'snap-shot' of social life is turned into a 'movie' (Leisering and Walker 1998: 265; Giele and Elder 1998; Berthoud

2000). While a snap-shot is created *synchronically*, in the moment, a movie develops *diachronically*, telling an unfolding story through time. However, temporal movies can be created in a rich variety of ways. How they are produced and what they tell us about social processes varies across different methodological traditions. Their similarities and differences rest on how they engage with two planes or flows of time:

**Prospective–retrospective (looking forwards, looking back).** This plane of time is concerned with how we orient ourselves to the past, present and future: prospectively (looking forwards), retrospectively (looking backwards) or both. In its purest form, longitudinal research is *prospective:* it follows the same people in 'real time' capturing changes and continuities as they occur and anticipating them in the future. A *retrospective* approach, on the other hand, explores dynamic processes through hindsight, a gaze backwards in time from the vantage point of the present day. In QL research, the temporal gaze may be directed forwards and backwards, oscillating between the two.

**Intensive–extensive (time frames and tempos).** This plane of time is concerned with the duration of temporal processes and the tempo of events: their spacing and regularity. For our purposes in this volume, the *time frame* of a QL study reflects the overall time span through which it is conducted, while its *tempo* reflects the number, duration and frequency of visits to the field. Taken together, time frames and tempos constitute the *longitudinal frame* of a QL study. A spectrum of approaches can be discerned: cases may be traced *intensively* via frequent or continuous visits to the field; or they may be traced *extensively* through regular, occasional or 'punctuated' revisits (Burawoy 2003) over many years or decades. In QL research, these two tempos may be combined as a study evolves.

These two flows of time form core elements in a framework for mapping time, which is set out in Chapter 2. They can be designed into QL research in flexible and creative ways, as Chapter 3 will show. QL researchers are likely to gaze both forwards and backwards in time, and may combine intensive and extensive tempos in their research designs. The discussion that follows outlines how these dimensions of time are used by researchers in their research designs. A third plane of time, the micro–macro plane, is also introduced below (and discussed further in Chapter 2). The mapping exercise begins with a consideration of longitudinal and life course research, before going on to consider the broader field of qualitative temporal enquiry.

## Longitudinal and life course research

Longitudinal research, whether quantitative or qualitative, is essentially prospective: it produces 'movies' that unfold in 'real' time, charting dynamic processes as they occur. While the focus of enquiry may straddle individuals, families, institutions or societies, the starting point for these studies is a micro-dynamic one; the same individuals, households or other collectives (known as a longitudinal 'panel' of participants) are tracked over the same periods of time. A panel study is synonymous with, and a good short hand for, a prospective longitudinal study. In discerning 'change in the making' (Mills 1959), these prospective designs are generally regarded as the purest form of longitudinal research (Ruspini 2002: 4).[2] They offer unique insights into dynamic processes, changes and continuities within the life course, between generations, and through history (Elliott 2005; Neale, Henwood and Holland 2012). Longitudinal studies commonly combine prospective tracking with a retrospective gathering of data on past times (Scott and Alwin 1998).

The life course provides a central organizing framework for the conduct of longitudinal panel studies. This is explored in more detail in Chapter 2, but some salient points are drawn out here. As the name implies, the focus is on how the course of a life unfolds through time. This can be understood *biologically* (an age-related process from birth to death), and/ or *biographically* (how a life is individually crafted and socially constructed from cradle to grave). It can also be understood *collectively* (how lives are

---

[2] In contrast to panel designs, repeated or recurrent cross-sectional designs gather and analyse group or population level data at each fieldwork visit (Ruspini 2002: 4; Grossoehme and Lipstein 2016). Since these designs do not follow the same samples they cannot discern changes in individual or collective biographies. However, the recruitment of different community, organizational or population samples at each wave enables an understanding of clusters of change in the social fabric. In some longitudinal studies, recurrent cross-sectional and panel designs are combined (see, for example, Loumidis and colleagues 2001).

shaped socially and institutionally within and across the generations), *historically* (the chronological times into which people are born and live out their lives), and *geographically* (the places and local cultures that give shape and form to unfolding lives). In other words, while individual biography is integral to life course research, so too is a concern with how lives unfold collectively, and how individual and collective lives shape and, in turn, are shaped by wider social processes (Elder 1994; Elder and Giele 2009).

The life course is a vital lynchpin for discerning the links between biography and history. The impetus for exploring these dual processes and their complex intersections was provided by Mills (1959), who saw this as the central challenge of the sociological imagination. His concern was to translate the personal troubles of biography into public issues of history and society:

> We cannot hope to understand society unless we have a prior understanding of the relationship between biography and history ... [the task is to] continually work out and revise your views on the problems of history, the problems of biography and the problems of social structure in which biography and history intersect. (Mills 1959: 225)

It is generally accepted among life course researchers that the complex intersection of these factors is best understood through a longitudinal lens. Yet, teasing out the varied factors that shape an unfolding life across the micro–macro plane is also a perennial challenge (see Chapter 2). How life course research is approached depends on how these domains of change are understood, and the relative priority accorded to them, creating a diverse and amorphous field of study (Neale 2015).

## Quantitative longitudinal research

Thus far our discussion has focused on the features that are common to longitudinal research, whether quantitative or qualitative. While both are prospective in their orientation to time, they operate at different scales of enquiry. This produces different kinds of movie, shaped by distinctive time frames and tempos. Quantitative longitudinal survey, cohort and panel studies began to develop in the United States in the late 1920s, primarily in the fields of medicine and child development, although on a smaller scale than contemporary studies (for overviews of developments see Phelps, Furstenberg and Colby 2002, and Ruspini 2002). These large-scale studies chart changes in patterns of social behaviour through the generation of big 'thin' data that can be analysed statistically, using event history modelling and other techniques (Elliott, Holland and Thomson 2008). The scale of these studies varies: a community-based study will recruit many hundreds of participants (e.g. the *Longitudinal Harlem Adolescent Health Study*, Brunswick 2002), while a nationally representative study (e.g. the 1958 cohort of the *National Child Development Study*) will recruit many thousands. Either way, these studies illuminate large-scale patterns of change based on very large datasets. Panel members are likely to be asked a series of semi-structured questions at regular intervals (typically every year for a longitudinal panel study, and five years for a birth cohort study, Ruspini 2002: 4). In general, then, tempos tend to be well regulated and extensive, with time frames stretching over several decades of change.

Given the scale of these studies, the focus tends to be on what changes, for whom, on the direction and extent of change and on where, when and how often change occurs. Data on the spells of time that people spend in particular states, for example, in the states of poverty or cohabitation, produce a broad, chronological picture of change across a study population (Leisering and Walker 1998). This creates a bird's-eye view of the social world, a 'long shot' that is panoramic in scope. The result is an *epic movie*, a highly valuable 'surface' picture of social dynamics. However, it is a movie in which the intricacies of the plot and the fluid twists and turns in the story line are hidden from view (Neale and Flowerdew 2003).

## Qualitative longitudinal research

QL research, in contrast, is located within the qualitative, interpretivist tradition (Ritchie and Lewis 2003). It has an equally venerable history. Van Gennep (1960 [1909]) was one of the earliest dynamic thinkers. In *The Rites of Passage* he conducted a secondary analysis of comparative data on the ritualized processes of birth, initiation into adulthood, marriage and death. This enabled him to develop insights into life course transitions that were in tune with local meanings and mechanisms of change. He was also one of the first anthropologists to establish the complex co-existence of continuity and change in the way lives unfold. A different kind of dynamic insight emerged from one of the earliest prospective QL studies, commissioned by the Fabian Society and set in Lambeth in London (Pember Reeves 2008 [1913]). In a study full of perceptive humanity, the researchers visited forty-two low-income working families on a weekly basis over the space of a year, documenting their budgets, diets, household conditions and health to reveal their changing family fortunes and precarious life chances.

In the mould of Pember Reeves's pioneering study, QL research typically takes the form of small-scale, in-depth studies of individuals or small collectives, tracking them intensively over relatively modest time frames to generate rich, situated, biographical data. The tempo for a QL study tends to be more intensive and flexible than its large-scale cousin: patterns of revisits vary, and each wave of data generation is used to inform the next (Smith 2003). A micro-dynamic focus is more deeply embedded in this form of longitudinal enquiry. Working from the individual or small collective 'upwards', the concern is not simply with those concrete events, changes and transitions that can be measured in precise ways, but with the agency of individuals in crafting these processes, the sensibilities and moral reasoning that underpin them, the strategies that people use to make sense of the past and navigate the future, and the local cultures which give shape to these processes.

In these ways, time is harnessed to the immediacy and vitality of human experience. QL research engages with human hearts and minds: it provides access to the 'interior logic' of lives, discerning how change is created, negotiated, lived and experienced. At the heart of this approach lies a concern with the dynamics of human agency – the capacity to act, to interact, to make choices, to influence the shape of one's life and the lives of others. Of equal importance is the dynamics of human subjectivity: the shifting meanings that events, circumstances and social processes hold for those who experience them (and, at the same time, acknowledging and engaging with the shifting subjectivities of researchers in their interpretations) (Thomson and colleagues 2002; McLeod and Thomson 2009). Midgely (2014) reminds us that these subjective facets of human experience are just as important for our verifications of the social world as any objectively defined fact or process. Subjective accounts are not fixed and the past is 'reworked' as people overwrite their biographies and strive for narrative coherence in their life stories (Kohli 1981; Halbwachs 1992; Neale and Flowerdew 2003; Cohler and Hostetler 2004; Holland and Thomson 2009).

By their very nature, then, agency and subjectivity are dynamic concepts, affording opportunities to discern changing perceptions, values, aspirations and strategies over time, alongside and in relation to concrete changes in events or circumstances. With its responsive tempo and sensibilities, QL research has been likened to the process of 'walking alongside' people as their lives unfold (Neale and Flowerdew 2003). Returning once more to the movie metaphor, QL research offers us an up-close-and-personal or *intimate movie*, providing insights into *how and why* the social world unfolds in varied ways, for specific individuals and collectives, in particular settings of change (Neale and Flowerdew 2003; Neale 2015). Being 'up close and personal' does entail some limitations. The depth of QL enquiry, the small sample sizes and the relatively modest time frames are likely to constrain the breadth of evidence and findings. And the longitudinal frame may not match or capture the momentum of a participant's life. Caveats may therefore be needed about the limited longitudinal reach of a study, and about how much it can reveal, particularly about longer-term trajectories and broader social processes of change.

The different kinds of longitudinal 'movie' outlined above have complementary strengths and weaknesses. Quantitative longitudinal research powerfully reveals the wholesale movement of study populations from one circumstance to another (e.g. into or out of the states of poverty, migration, marriage or ill health). QL research, in turn, has the potential to reveal why such journeys are undertaken, the factors that shape the journey, and how they are managed and experienced. Are continued states bound up with stability, inertia or stagnation? How do transitions and trajectories unfold (upward or downward, stable or volatile, running in parallel or inter-connecting)? How and why do these pathways converge or diverge across the cases in a sample? Is a journey planned or sudden, prescribed or imposed, joyous or traumatic? Is a transition a smooth and positive one, or are there detours and setbacks along with way? QL research has the capacity to address these intricate dynamic questions and to produce plausible accounts of the generative mechanisms and processes through which changes occur (Elliott 2005). Much like Homer's Odyssey, the nature and meaning of the journey assumes just as much importance as the destination reached (Neale 2015).

Some of the most perceptive insights on the value of QL research come from life course researchers whose work straddles both traditions:

> While demographic surveys show the magnitude and distribution of migration in entire populations ... only individual or family histories can reveal why one individual moves and another stays put. (Giele 2009: 236)

Although quantitative longitudinal research has the potential to provide very detailed information about individuals, what is lost in this approach ... are the narratives that individuals tell about their own lives. ... The narrative approach allows for a more active, processual view of identity that shifts over time and is more context dependent. ... Quantitative research can never provide access to the reflexive individual. ... Without this element there is a danger that people are merely seen as making decisions and acting within a predefined and structurally determined field of social relations, rather than contributing to both the maintenance and metamorphosis of the culture and community in which they live. (Elliott 2005: 131)

Perhaps the most compelling evidence in support of these statements comes from individuals who have participated in both forms of enquiry. The following reflections are from panel members in the large-scale *National Child Development Study* (*NCDS 1958 Cohort*) who, at the age of fifty, took part in an innovative qualitative wave of the research (Elliott 2010a: 3–4):

The researcher comes, and they take the information from you. Sometimes it's just a question of a yes or no ... and I might want to put a maybe there ... or something. And there's sort of areas where you think, 'oh, but they don't ask me that'. And, I think, 'they should know that' ... so this [life interview] for me is good 'cause I've been able to sort of say to you things that have gone on in my life that perhaps the NCDS haven't known about.

I have been quite open and [said] things ... to you that I probably haven't told a lot of other people. But you've probably got a picture now of what ... sort of person I'm like from that, and if you got somebody coming to your home every few years and ... asking some questions and going again, they're not getting to know the real person.

## Bridging the gap

Quantitatively-led longitudinal studies have traditionally been seen as the 'gold standard' of life course research, while QL research has been cast in a more peripheral role: as a useful supplement to the broader studies that 'resides on the margins of mainstream life course research' (Heinz

2003: 75; Elder and Giele 2009: vii–viii). Among life course researchers, particularly in the United States, knowledge of the growing corpus of QL research remains limited; and it continues to be cast as a fledgling approach that lacks clear definition or any grounding in established methodological traditions (see, for example, Hermanowicz 2016). Nonetheless, it is increasingly recognized that these two forms of longitudinal enquiry create equally valuable and complementary visions of the social world. Many of the issues faced by longitudinal researchers are common to those working in both traditions, creating a forum for a productive cross-fertilization of ideas and insights (Phelps, Furstenberg and Colby 2002; Elliott, Holland and Thomson 2008). There is, too, a growing interest in ways to bridge the gap between them. Scaled-down community level surveys are developing that are no longer driven by the search for elusive, nationally representative samples (Rothman, Gallacher and Hatch 2013). Mixed longitudinal methodologies are being refined (Laub and Sampson 1998; Heinz 2003), while QL methods are increasingly nested within or used to complement larger scale studies (e.g. Entwisle, Alexander and Olson 2002; Farrell and colleagues 2006; Elliott, Miles, Parsons and Savage 2010; Morrow and Crivello 2015). The potential to work across these traditions in a narrative approach to social enquiry also represents a significant advance (Cohler and Hostetler 2004; Elliott 2005).

In a parallel development, while QL research is traditionally equated with small-scale, situated enquiries, recent initiatives have seen a 'scaling up' of QL research in ways that can enhance the evidence base and combine depth with breadth of data and analysis. One line of development involves revisiting and combining existing data drawn from varied QL or mixed longitudinal datasets (Lindsey, Metcalfe and Edwards 2015). This was one of the aims of the *Timescapes Study*, which brought together and archived seven QL projects to facilitate their collective reuse (Bishop and Neale 2010; Neale and Bishop 2012; Irwin, Bornat and Winterton 2012; Irwin and Winterton 2014; www.timescapes.leeds.ac.uk).

The development of Qualitative Panel Research (QPR or QPS) represents another way to extend the scope of a QL study (Burton, Purvin and Garrett-Peters 2009; Morrow and Crivello 2015; the Welfare Conditionality Study www.welfareconditionality.ac.uk). These studies are by no means small-scale in terms of sample size, geographical coverage, team composition and/or historical reach. In effect, they represent a third kind of movie, *intimate epics*, which are grounded in big 'rich' data and evidence, yet, crucially, retain their depth and explanatory power (Neale 2015). These attempts to bridge the gap between these two longitudinal traditions are relatively new developments, but they suggest the rise of a new and enriched methodological infrastructure within which longitudinal and life course research can advance and flourish.

## Mapping developments in qualitative temporal research

Our discussion now turns to a consideration of qualitative temporal studies. We begin with social anthropological field research and go on to consider sociological re-studies, and biographical, oral historical and narrative forms of research. The aim here is to tease out the ways that these established fields of scholarship engage with time, and to discern the place of QL enquiry within them. It is worth noting that the common threads within these fields of study tend to outweigh their differences; there are many parallel developments across these fields and a significant cross-fertilization of methodological ideas and insights.

### Longitudinal ethnography

Social anthropologists have been conducting ethnographic research in small-scale, agrarian communities since the early twentieth century (Foster and colleagues 1979; Peterson Royce and Kemper 2002). Many such studies are conducted longitudinally. The approach typically involves continuous, intensive ethnographic immersion (a mixture of participant-observation and interviews), followed by a more extensive engagement, sometimes over many decades of revisits, by the same researcher (and, often, thereafter, by new generations of researchers who 'inherit' a particular field site). This produces a distinctive longitudinal frame. In the tradition of Marcel Mauss, Howell (2012: 156) likens the process to dipping 'different nets in a teeming ocean, each time producing a different catch'. She stresses, too, that the constituent elements of the ocean are transformed over time, and that informed ethnographers throw their metaphorical nets purposively rather than randomly, based on informed understandings of shifting local terrains (2012: 157).

Longitudinal ethnographies are essentially prospective in nature, with revisits anticipated and planned for. But they also entail a constant retrospective gaze, made possible through the longer-term historical reach of the studies. The combination of ethnography with an extensive historical reach is, perhaps, the most distinctive and impressive feature of these studies when compared to the more modest time frames that usually characterize QL studies. Longitudinal ethnographers are able to explore how lives are being *lived* as well as narrated, and how both lived and narrated lives change through time. Serial re-studies in these evolving communities, conducted by the same or a different researcher after a lapse of many years, are also common (reviewed in Burawoy 2003). Whether anthropological field research is 'truly' longitudinal (i.e. involving a continuous or regular field engagement) or a re-study (after a gap of many years), the focus tends to be on the changing community itself rather than individuals or small collectives within. Nevertheless, the small scale of traditional communities and the intensive engagement means that anthropologists develop a micro-dynamic knowledge of the lives of community members, particularly of their key informants, with whom they often develop close and enduring ties.

Research carried out by Foster (1979, 2002) in the Mexican village of Tzintzuntzan is a prime example. The baseline phase of fieldwork, conducted in 1945–6, comprised six months of continuous ethnography, followed by monthly visits each lasting a week. Twelve years later, in 1957, Foster revisited the community once again, and thereafter became committed to a life-time of regular revisits (once or twice a year) that spanned half a century of change (Foster 1979, 2002). As Foster notes, his study bridges the gap between a continuous longitudinal field engagement and a more punctuated re-study, and he was able to look forwards and backwards in time to discern the impact of historical developments on the lives of the villagers. Like many long-term anthropologists, Foster developed an enduring commitment to the community he revisited, and, upon his retirement, 'passed the mantle' to a new generation of researchers (Foster 1979, 2002; Peterson Royce and Kemper 2002).

The power to discern dynamic processes through longitudinal ethnography was initially slow to develop. While early empiricists visited the field on numerous occasions, they produced a series of snap-shots that had no temporal connection (Foster and colleagues 1979; Burawoy 2003; Howell and Talle 2012). The concern was to document bounded, 'traditional' societies, through an extended 'ethnographic present'. This was so much taken for granted that the historical moment when data were gathered was deemed irrelevant and the dates rarely recorded

(Foster and colleagues 1979: 4; Fabian 1983; Peterson Royce and Kemper 2002).

This began to change in the post-war years in response to a growing awareness that 'models of society that leave out time are inadequate ... our concern is not *whether* to study change, but *how* to study it' (Wilson 1977: 21). There was a growing need to acknowledge the dynamic and open-ended nature of social systems and to develop methodologies that could capture these processes (Firth 1959; Foster and colleagues 1979). From the late 1970s, longitudinal ethnography began to advance through a series of edited collections that explored how lives could be studied 'through the stream of time' (Kemper and Peterson Royce, 2002: xv). There is an enduring appeal in the use of longitudinal ethnography, or what Grandia (2015) has recently called 'slow' ethnography, for in combining qualitative depth with historical reach it represents one of the most powerful forms of QL enquiry. The foundations of QL research lie predominantly in the pioneering work of longitudinal ethnographers, who have laid the groundwork for its advancement in recent decades.

## Sociological re-studies

The ethnographic tradition described above fed directly into the development of sociological re-studies in industrial societies. These began to appear in varied community settings in the first half of the twentieth century. As the name implies, a re-study involves revisiting and updating an earlier study to discover new insights about the past in relation to the present day. Newly generated data are brought into dialogue with the findings and data from an earlier study, creating the means for a direct comparison between the two (for comprehensive reviews see Bell and Newby 1971; Crow 2002, 2012; Charles and Crow 2012). Duncan (2012: 313) describes these studies as a 'sort of comparative research, but using comparisons over time, instead of over space'.

It is possible to trace a long line of re-study scholarship, from the serial studies of 'Middletown' (the American city of Muncie), to contemporary re-studies in the town of Swansea (Lynd and Lynd 1929, 1937; Lassiter 2012; Rosser and Harris 1965; Charles, Davies and Harris 2008). In what was seen as a productive fusion of anthropological and sociological methods, the earlier studies often included researchers from both traditions, used a mixture of ethnographic and interview-based methods, and focused on communities as the unit of study. At the same time, they were pioneering a particular form of historical sociology that was being promoted more broadly within the social sciences (Mills 1959; Gergen 1973; Abrams 1982):

> Sociology without history resembles a Hollywood set: great scenes, sometimes brilliantly painted, with nothing and nobody behind them. (Tilly, cited in Miller 2000: 21)

From the outset, there was an overriding concern with the intersecting processes of social change and continuity (the latter often framed at that time in terms of 'tradition'). This concern was not confined to the re-studies themselves but was also a preoccupation of the original researchers (see, for example, Stacey 1960).

The particular way in which early re-studies engaged with time has given this field a distinctive character. Firstly, re-studies rarely seek to build understandings prospectively, tracing dynamic processes as they occur. While longitudinal ethnographies combine a prospective and retrospective gaze, here the gaze is retrospective, looking backwards to compare two snap-shots in time, the past and the present day. Secondly, unlike longitudinal ethnographies, which may combine intensive and extensive tempos, re-studies are extensive. The original study and the re-study are typically separated by many years (at least a decade), creating significant historical reach. The backward gaze, the extensive reach over time and the community focus of these studies means that the same individuals are rarely followed. This limits the scope to discern how lives are unfolding biographically, or how biographical and historical processes intersect.[3] Overall, these studies have traditionally been marked by a pronounced break in continuity between the original research and the re-study. This tends to be reinforced where anthropological or sociological re-studies are carried out by second-generation researchers, who enter the field armed with a fresh, untrammelled vision (although, where possible, there will be some collaboration or at least consultation with the original researchers; see, for example, Lewis 1951 and Charles, Davies and Harris 2008).

Overall, the particular strength of re-studies lies in their extensive tempo, bringing macro-historical processes into sharp relief, and enabling

---

[3] Although researchers may well attempt to trace the original participants where these are known (see, for example, Stacey, Batstone, Bell and Murcott 1975; and further studies reviewed in Crow 2012).

these processes to be re-visioned through a reflexive, retrospective gaze. However, re-studies carried out in this way cannot create the processual understanding that a prospective longitudinal frame would allow. Linked to this, there is less scope to follow the same individuals and thereby build a biographical understanding of change into the picture. In these dimensions of temporal design, re-studies and QL studies tend to have different strengths and weaknesses.

However, the way re-studies engage with time is not set in stone. The potential to fuse re-study methodology with elements of QL enquiry is ripe for development, and is nicely illustrated in the historical/sociological comparative research of O'Connor and Goodwin (2010, 2012) and Goodwin and O'Connor (2015). Since 2001, these researchers have been re-studying the *Leicester Young Workers Study*, which had been conducted by Norbert Elias and his colleagues in the early 1960s. A rich dataset had been generated, based on an interview-based survey with nearly 900 young adults, and including contact details of the participants. Unfortunately, the research was never completed. For some forty years, this treasure trove of data languished in a large number of box files in an attic storeroom in the Department of Sociology at the University of Leicester, before it was re-discovered, reconstituted and re-purposed. The researchers were able to 'read' the data from the earlier study in new ways, and shed fresh light on the precarious employment experiences of young people in the 1960s, thereby filling a major gap in our knowledge of youth employment and unemployment in post-war Britain (Goodwin and O'Connor 2015). They also used the original study as a baseline for a new study of youth transitions and employment in Leicester, generating fresh insights on changing practices and circumstances over historical time.

Of particular significance for our discussion here, the researchers were also able to trace, re-interview and reconstruct the biographies of a hundred people from the original sample, retrospectively building a more processual understanding of the employment trajectories of their participants over four decades. This micro-dynamic data not only afforded some continuity from past to present, but enabled historical processes to be anchored in and understood through the changing personal lives of the participants (Goodwin and O'Connor 2015). In this way, a synchronic dataset, generated at a particular historical moment, was turned into an extensive, QL dataset spanning a period of forty years (O'Connor and Goodwin 2010, 2012: 486). As the authors note, there is huge and as yet untapped potential to build QL re-studies in the future. This would require a greater focus on the unfolding lives of individuals and, more pragmatically, the ability to identify and trace the original participants in a study. In turn, this relies on a commitment to preserve and archive the original unabridged datasets, complete with participant contact details, for the use of future generations of researchers.

## Biographical, oral history and narrative research

Our mapping exercise concludes with a consideration of a group of cognate disciplines that are centrally concerned with the unfolding biographies of individuals or small collectives. In this, they share a common endeavour with life course research, albeit their methods for engaging with time tend to differ. Bornat (2004: 34) usefully observes,

> The turn to biography in social science … coupled with a … grudging acceptance of the contribution of memory in historical research, has resulted in a proliferation of terms, schools, and groupings, often used interchangeably, some with a disciplinary base, others attempting to carve out new territory between disciplines. Labels such as oral history, biography, life story, life history, narrative analysis, reminiscence and life review jostle and compete for attention. What is common to all is a focus on recording and interpreting … the life experiences of individuals. (Bornat 2004: 34)

Biographical research evolved within the sociology of industrial societies, notably the Chicago school in the 1920s and 1930s (Thomas and Znaniecki, (1958) [1918–21]; Shaw 1966 [1930]). Thereafter it fell quickly into decline, but was subsequently revived in the post-war years. Since that time it has gradually coalesced into a recognized field of qualitative research, with global reach and influence. While precise methods vary, the approach involves the biographical and narrative construction and analysis of individual lives (or significant dimensions of these lives), which are then placed within a nexus of micro-social connections, historical events and processes, and life experiences (Miller 2000).[4] While these studies use a rich fusion of sociology and history, this is history 'from below' (Perks and

---

[4] Key texts include Thompson (2000), Bertaux (1981), Denzin (1989), Chamberlayne, Bornat and Wengraf (2000), Miller (2000), Plummer (2001), Roberts (2002), Andrews, Squire and Tamboukou (2008) and O'Neill et al. (2015).

Thomson 2016). The aim is to encourage the creative, interpretive story-telling of lives in ways that remain close to the experiences of those under study, and that views socio-historical processes from their perspective (Roberts 2002; Andrews 2008). These developments in the post-war years were driven by a desire to counter the growing dominance of positivist social survey research in the social sciences, which, in its concern with broad patterns of human behaviour, simply erased individuals from the historical record (Bertaux 1981). Thomas and Znaniecki (1958 [1918–21]) were, perhaps, the first to establish the value of subjective accounts as a source of meaning and insight, but the message has been reinforced by each new generation of researchers (see, for example, Portelli 2016 [1979]).

At the same time, and taking their lead from Mills (1959), these studies share with life course research a strong focus on the intersection of micro- and macro-historical processes, moving from the particular to the general, and maintaining the integrity of the former while elaborating on the latter (Bertaux 1981; Denzin 1989; Miller 2000; Andrews 2007). As Miller (2000: 22) notes, life stories cannot be told without a constant reference to historical change. Such studies often draw together a range of documentary and archival sources, generated at different historical moments, to create a more holistic picture. Thomas and Znaniecki (1958 [1918–21]), for example, drew on letters, newspaper reports and autobiographical records that were solicited by the researchers for their pioneering study of Polish immigrants. This tradition continues today in the work of the Mass Observation Archive, which has for many years commissioned personal accounts on varied aspects of life from a panel of volunteer reporters (www.massobs. org.uk see, for example, Broad and Fleming 1981). Thompson (1981: 290) observes that social biographers and oral historians are 'jackdaws' rather than methodological purists, 'bricoleurs' who are adept at teasing out a variety of evidence to piece together a richer, composite picture of lives and times.[5] The agenda, then, has been to create a people's history through oral testimony (Thompson 1981); to bring subjective life histories to bear on an understanding of socio-historical processes (Bertaux 1981; Hareven 2000);

---

[5] The idea of bricolage was first introduced by Levi-Strauss (1966) and is perfectly suited to these biographical fields of study. It is the skill of using whatever materials are at hand and re-combining them in a patchwork or montage of evidence to create new insights (Yardley 2008: 12).

and to establish and validate a humanistic, processual approach to social science enquiry (Plummer 2001).

While these fields of biographical research have different methodological inflections, they tend to engage with time in similar ways. Firstly, they tend to reconstruct life histories through a retrospective gaze rather than prospectively tracing lives through time. The personal accounts of individuals are used to anchor researcher reconstructions of the past. Linked to this retrospective gaze, temporal data are usually gathered synchronically, through a single visit to the field, rather than diachronically, through time (Miller 2000: 40). This makes design easier and cheaper to manage, and it perhaps also explains the preoccupation with capturing lives through life history or narrative styles of interviewing. Yet it does not allow for a processual understanding of dynamic processes as they evolve. The way time has been utilized within these studies creates a divergence with QL enquiry. But, as we have seen for re-studies, these differences are not set in stone. Like all qualitative temporal researchers, social biographers and oral historians are creative and adaptable. The field has evolved to become, 'a vast and constantly changing and expanding ferment of creative work ... [that] thrives on invention' (Bornat 2008: 344). This has resulted in some exciting fusions of biographical, oral historical and QL designs, and the development of what has recently been called *longitudinal biography* (King and Roberts 2015). For example, working as part of the *Timescapes Study*, Bornat and Bytheway developed a panel design for *The Oldest Generation Study* (Bornat and Bytheway 2008, 2010, Bytheway 2011). The researchers were able to explore biographies prospectively, looking forwards as well as backwards in time, and they rose to the challenge of discerning how those living in deep old age both perceive and 'live out' the future for themselves and their families.

### Concluding reflections

In this introductory chapter, the place of QL enquiry has been explored in relation to the established canons of longitudinal and life course research, and the key disciplines that make up the field of qualitative temporal research. In the process, some of its distinctive features have been sharpened, not least its capacity to discern how biographies unfold in 'real' time, through a rich, prospective, qualitative lens. An appreciation of these features has grown rapidly over the past two decades, enabling QL research to take a more established place within the temporal canon. There is evidence too of some creative synergies between these different fields of enquiry. As we have seen, in longitudinal research there is an emerging interest in working across and bridging the divide between large- and smaller-scale studies. At the same time, researchers conducting sociological re-studies and biographical research are exploring the interface of their own disciplinary traditions and QL research, and consciously engaging with the latter as a way to frame their enquiries (see, for example, O'Reilly 2012; O'Connor and Goodwin 2010, 2012; Stanley 2013, 2015; King and Roberts 2015).

Mapping the fields of longitudinal and temporal research in this chapter has illustrated some of the subtle differences and commonalities that exist between varied modes of temporal enquiry. The discussion suggests the value of working across the spectrum, blending different methodological traditions in a creative approach to research design. These are porous fields of research, with a great deal of cross-fertilization between them, and scope for much more. In this respect, QL research defies prescriptive labelling and neat categorization. QL researchers are consummate bricoleurs. They borrow liberally from the longitudinal and re-study fields to fashion the designs and tempos for their research, and adopt ethnographic, biographical and narrative approaches to generating data in order to create the necessary depth of temporal understanding. While QL research requires rigour, it is also a craft, involving the application of a repertoire of strategies to fashion a bespoke design (Saldana 2003). This theme is developed further in Chapter 3, but, before this, our exploration of QL research takes us on a journey through time.

# 2 Conceptual foundations: Rethinking time and the life course

## Introduction

The notion that QL research has the capacity for a rich engagement with time raises questions about how that engagement actually occurs. In this chapter we take up this theme. The reader is taken on a short journey through time to explore the conceptual underpinnings for QL research. Two broad ways of conceptualizing time are outlined here: *fixed*, linear time, the realm of the clock and calendar and *fluid* multidimensional time, the realm of temporality. This distinction is recognized in all fields of temporal research, and is nicely reflected in the everyday metaphors that are used to make time tangible. On the one hand, spatial metaphors (life journeys, passages, transitions, pathways etc.) capture the sense of lives unfolding chronologically through time, with an implied purpose and direction of travel.[1] On the other hand, the imagery of waves, streams, flows, drops and ripples usefully captures the perpetual movement and fluidity of time. In its vastness and ever-present motion, time has been likened to an ocean (Saldana 2003: 5).

Taking both fixed and fluid understandings of time into account is a necessary foundation for QL research design and practice. Time becomes more than a methodological strategy, the medium through which QL research is conducted (however important that is). In its fluid

---

[1] The use of spatial metaphors, however, should not be taken to imply linearity and orderly sequences. These journeys may be more akin to the wanderings of Odysseus and other iconic and eternal travellers who appear throughout the great literature, oral traditions, art and music of the world.

dimensions, time can also be understood as a rich theoretical category and topic of enquiry that drives the generation and analysis of QL data. It is this latter conception of time, *time as topic*, as opposed to *time as vehicle*, which is the focus here. The discussion explores five ways to map time, followed by a consideration of the temporal dimensions of the life course and its conceptual building blocks. The overall aim is to explore how time, as a rich theoretical category, can feed into and enrich empirical investigation.[2]

## Rethinking time

Studying lives through time seems, at first glance, to be self-evident and straightforward, a matter of creating a moving, chronological picture that charts observable changes and discerns what happens next. This approach rests on conventional understandings of time as an empirical, linear construct, tied to the clock and calendar. Yet lives do not necessarily unfold in chronological order, through discrete stages, in one linear direction or at a uniform pace. Nor do people experience time in these linear ways (Strauss 1997 [1959]: 93; Kelly and McGrath 1988: 55). Time can also be perceived as a non-linear, multidimensional social construct that shapes and, in turn, is shaped through lived experiences. Such ideas are hardly new. They have been developed over the decades through a wealth of socio-historical and temporal theorizing (see, for example, Mannheim 1952 [1927]). The discussion here draws primarily on the work of Barbara Adam (1990).

Adam (1990) draws a fundamental distinction between 'fixed' and 'fluid' time, in much the same way that Aristotle distinguishes between impersonal, atomistic time (chronos) and flowing, value-laden time (kairos) (Chaplin 2002). She explains that most of our social scientific and common-sense assumptions about time are reflected in clock and calendar time. Time is perceived as an invariant, chronological, linear feature of life, a quantity that is objective and measurable, with a relentless, regular and recurrent motion that is expressed numerically. Paradoxically, 'fixed' time has two intertwined dimensions: it is inexorably advancing and irreversible (a river that flows to the sea), yet it recurs in repetitive cycles (the perpetual

---

[2] The discussion in this chapter draws on and develops themes that were first introduced in Neale (2015).

wheel of time). Past and future are separate and identical realms, held apart by the progression of the clock. Time in this formulation provides an external structure within which our lives are measured, planned, organized and regulated. The assumption is that people experience time in a uniform way. In the process, time becomes a resource, a commodity and a site of power and control. Under 'clock' time, then, lives progress and events occur *in time*, for time is external to them. Time becomes a shared background, a taken-for-granted presence, the constant and unvarying medium through which lives are lived and events unfold.

This view of time is a recent social construction within Western industrial societies, yet it is pervasive and of global significance, making it difficult to think beyond or outside it. Time is so extensively embodied in the mechanics of the clock that the clock *becomes* time. Yet this model of time has its source in outmoded forms of scientific explanation and logic (Newtonian physics). Drawing on more recent scientific advances (relativity theory, quantum physics, chaos theory and ecological biology) Adam offers a powerful way to rethink and transcend clock time, turning our common sense notions of time on their head to consider not events *in time*, but *time in* events. In this fluid realm of temporality, time has a kaleidoscopic quality. It is not fixed but fluid, rhythmically and perpetually emerging in multidimensional ways in varied local contexts. Objective, constant, one-dimensional clock time gives way to a plurality of times, held in a simultaneous relationship with each other, flowing and intersecting in complex and unpredictable ways. Past and future, for example, are no longer separate states that progress chronologically, in a linear direction; they are processes that flow into one another, suggesting that our understandings of the past are no more fixed than the future. These flows of time are embedded within our day-to-day lives; they are embodied, subjective and context dependent, inhering in and emerging from our social events and practices. In all their complexity and flux, social practices and events do not occur *in time*; they *constitute* time. Time becomes our creation.

Seeing time in this way transforms our understandings of change and causality. In clock time our focus is on what happens from one point in time to the next. Change is seen as an instrumental, concrete, linear process, and its study an empirical matter of charting and documenting processes and events in chronological sequence. Similarly, causality is implied in the linear, orderly progression from past to present to future; cause and effect are intimately tied to this sense of chronology.

However, change and causal processes can also be understood in a fluid way: as subjectively defined, situated phenomena that are integral to the world of experience and which pervade all life processes. Seen in this way, complex causal processes defy prediction; they are best discerned retrospectively, by looking backwards and reconstructing past lives from the vantage point of the present day (Laub and Sampson 2003; Andrews 2008). They also defy simple, unitary explanations that link past events with future outcomes. Causality cannot be traced back to a single identifiable moment or event. It is the accumulation of multiple events or experiences, and their complex configurations that assume significance (Pettigrew 1995; Saldana 2003: 8-12). Causal processes emerge in specific contexts of time and place, inviting consideration of the multiple generative mechanisms through which life course changes occur (a theme developed further below).[3] Overall, then, these dynamic processes emerge within and derive their meaning from the social practices and unfolding contexts in which they are embedded (Saldana 2003). In contrasting 'fixed' and 'fluid' time, Adam stresses that these are not either/or formulations. Both need to be taken into account as empirical realities that influence everyday existence. Even so, in the broader, more fluid formulation offered by Adam, narrowly conceived clock time loses its dominance. It becomes one among many complex flows of time that make up our temporal world. The key task then becomes a holistic one: to discern and investigate the flows and rhythms of time and, crucially, to explore the webs of their intrinsic connections, how they are implicated in each other.

Adam's contribution is far reaching. She creates an alternative vision of the nature of temporal reality, an alternative ontology of time. Nearly three decades on, some progress has been made to import these insights into empirical social science. Yet, perhaps understandably, clock time continues to dominate life course and longitudinal research, particularly in the quantitative tradition. Time remains a self-evident, empirical dimension of research. A moving, chronological picture of progressions from 'stage' to 'stage' emerges through the simple expedient of building calendar time in as the medium for conducting a study and the basis for comparison. Indeed, these strategies are used in all longitudinal studies. But QL research

---

[3] A detailed discussion of causality and its use in qualitative enquiry is beyond the scope of this book. Among many insightful accounts, see Abbott 2001 and Elliott 2005.

is also centrally concerned with fluid time, the complex flows of time in human experience. Time as a rich theoretical and social construct becomes a topic of enquiry that drives the formulation of research questions, and enriches the content and analysis of QL data.

## Timescapes: Flows of time

Temporal theorists classify time in a rich variety of ways (see, for example, the varied flows of time identified by Nowotny (1994) and Flaherty (2011), who distinguishes between duration, frequency, sequence, timing etc.). For our purposes here, time is mapped along five intersecting planes. While these are porous and flow into each other, they are separated out here to illuminate the interface between temporal theory and research practice, and to provide a foundation for empirical investigation:

- Prospective–retrospective: looking forwards, looking back
- Intensive–extensive: time frames and tempos
- Micro–macro: the scales of time
- Time–space: the spatial dimensions of time
- Continuous–discontinuous: the synchronicities of time

These planes or flows of time have theoretical value, as rich topics of enquiry and analysis, as well as methodological value, feeding into study design. It is their theoretical potential which is the main focus of attention here.

## Prospective–retrospective: Looking forwards, looking back

This plane of time is foundational in discerning the dynamic unfolding of lives and the way we orient ourselves to time. As shown in Chapters 1 and 3, looking forwards, prospectively, and looking backwards, retrospectively, are basic approaches that may be combined in the design of a QL study. Our concern here is with the theoretical dimensions of these processes. Fixed time focuses our attention on the chronology of past–present–future, seen as a linear construct that proceeds in one direction and in an orderly sequence. It invites consideration of people's life journeys, the markers and vantage points that locate them on their way, where they have come from, where they are heading (the direction of travel and sequencing of events), and what propels them onwards or holds them back. This is the basic framework commonly used in biographical interviewing (see Chapter 5).

In the fluid realm of temporality, however, the relationship between past, present and future is more complex. The temporal gaze is continually shifting as people look back and forth in the ever-moving present, overwriting their biographies, reinterpreting wider social and structural forces and confounding any sense of chronology and the orderly sequencing of events. Saldana (2003: 7, citing Jean-Luc Godard) notes that 'a story should have a beginning, a middle and an ending, but not necessarily in that order'. Moreover, past, present and future are simultaneously present and interacting at any one moment in time, and are continually under construction and reconstruction as the temporal gaze shifts. They emerge as interlocking flows of time that are in constant conversation with one another (Hardgrove, Rootham and McDowell 2015). Understanding how individuals shape their biographies through the fluid stream of time becomes just as important as understanding transitions through fixed chronologies:

> Invariably the stories we tell about ourselves, as well as those to which we attend as audience, are always ... anchored on shifting ground. ... We are forever re-scripting our pasts, making sense of the things that happened. This is true not only as narrators of our own lives, but also as narrators of the lives of others. This process of re-interpretation of events is one that is ongoing throughout our lives, as different parts of our past reveal themselves to hold increased importance, or to be void of meaning, depending not only on who we are, but critically, on whom we wish to become. (Andrews 2008: 94)

> Every narrative about [the] past is always also a story told in and about the present, as well as a story about the future. This ... is much like the temporal structure of human life itself. ... Understanding a life is understanding the continuous oscillating of ... past, present and future. (Brockmeier 2000, cited in Andrews 2008: 94)

For QL researchers, revisiting past and future at each research encounter is a powerful way to understand these shifting processes (see recursive interviewing in Chapter 5). The process invites consideration of narrative change, changes in perception and the presentation of a life, as well as chronological change (Lewis 2007). In two recent QL studies, Helen, a young child, and Elizabeth, a woman of retirement age, give compelling accounts of how they came to understand their past lives in a new light (Neale and Flowerdew 2007: 37; Andrews 2008: 87). Such evidence lends weight to Kierkegaard's (1843) famous observation that while life must be lived forwards in time, it can only be understood backwards (cited in Andrews 2008). The past, seen as hindsight, memory, heritage, legacies, reputations and so on, becomes a powerful, subjective resource that plays an important role in life planning, the ongoing construction of social identities and the shaping of moral lives (Freeman 2010).

The future, meanwhile, is a neglected site of research, yet it inheres in and shapes every day realities, and has the potential to reveal the nature of aspirations and the seeds of change (Adam and Groves 2007). For example, the extent to which people engage in life planning (the idea of 'choice' biographies) or live in an extended present which curtails their capacity to think about the long term, much less plan for it, are important topics of enquiry (Nowotny 1994). Brannen and Nilsen (2002) suggest that young people orient themselves to the future in three different ways: deferment, which keeps the future at bay; adaptability, which forges a future by responding to contingencies; and predictability, which strives for certainty and security over time. Concepts such as these have provided the foundation for a range of studies of youth transitions (see, for example, Henderson and colleagues 2007).

Imaginary futures are important topics of biographical enquiry (detailed in Chapter 5). Krings and colleagues (2013), for example, found that how their participants viewed the future in 2010 substantially differed from how they saw it in 2008, when their study began. Future accounts are usually seen as reflections of where people are on their life journeys at the moment in which the accounts are elicited. In other words, they are understood to have little or no predictive or causal power (Sanders and Munford 2008; Elliott 2010b; Hardgrove, Rootham and McDowell 2015). However, they may have motivational power, the propensity to bring into focus possible future selves, the notion of 'becoming', and thereby to shape, nurture and strengthen inner biographical dispositions (Strauss 1997 [1959]; Hardgrove, Rootham and McDowell 2015; Worth 2009). Arguably, how people orient themselves to the future may influence the paths they take, for people cannot work towards future aspirations unless they have the capacity to imagine them (Hardgrove, Rootham and McDowell 2015; Worth 2009). In this way, the conjuring of an imaginary future may become a trigger point for change (a theme discussed further below and in Chapter 5):

> There is, for the adolescent, the demand, or at least the opportunity to direct his thoughts both behind and ahead of the present moment; swinging rapidly from one perspective to another, comparing, predicting, regretting and resolving afresh; planning for the future but preserving continuity with the present; making the best of what has been, ensuring the best of what could come. (Veness 1962: 2)

## Intensive–extensive: Time frames and tempos

As shown in Chapter 1, this plane of time is central to QL methodology: it shapes the time frame (the overall time span) for a study, and the tempo (the number, length and frequency) of visits to the field. However, this plane of time also has rich theoretical potential. Time frames and tempos afford rich possibilities for uncovering the experiential dimensions of life course processes: the acuteness or chronicity of change, and whether time is perceived intensively, in the moment, or extensively, stretching over longer-term horizons. Life states, for example, may be perceived as fleeting or enduring, temporary or permanent, while individuals may oscillate between change and continuity, action and inaction as their lives unfold. The work of enduring hardship or sustaining relationships, how people bide their time, is another important dimension of this plane of time. Alheit (1994), for example, identifies two contrasting time horizons in the life course: *everyday time*, which is cyclical and involves spontaneity as well as routine, and *life-time*, longer-term horizons that are retrospectively constructed in linear and sequential terms. How individuals reconcile these different horizons of time in making sense of their lives is a fruitful line of enquiry.

Closely allied to the tempo of time is its pace: our experiences of the rhythms, repetitions and velocity of time, the speed at which time is perceived to pass and whether it is slowing down or accelerating. The pace of time emerges in varied ways, for example, across the generations, where the pace of young childhood or deep old age is noticeably slower than the pace of youth or adulthood. Similarly, the speed and suddenness of change, and whether multiple changes occur in quick succession, are important dimensions of lived experience, inviting consideration of how change processes are managed (Flowerdew and Neale 2003). As a final example, time use and work–life balance studies, both qualitative and quantitative, have flourished over past decades. These are driven by a concern that life is speeding up and becoming more routinized, regulated and frenetic in industrial society (Crow and Heath 2002; Rosa 2013; Wajcman 2015; Gershuny 2000 and related studies from the *Oxford Centre for Time Use Research*).

Studies of this temporal plane often distinguish between industrial time (the rigid, impersonal tempo of the clock: Aristotle's *chronos*), and family, personal or holiday time (which is fluid, flexible, enduring and value laden: Aristotle's kairos) (Hareven 1982). Chaplin (2002) and Harden and colleagues (2012), for example, have explored how families oscillate between and manage these two contrasting tempos in their daily lives. Finally, Lemke (2000) suggests we simultaneously inhabit a whole spectrum of time horizons, from the microscopic (where time is incomprehensible because it is fleeting and moves at lightning speed), to the cosmic (where time is incomprehensible because it is infinite and appears to stand still). The different horizons of turning points, transitions and trajectories (explored below) are embedded within this grand, cosmic scheme.

## Micro–macro: The scales of time

The centrality of this plane of time within temporal research was established in Chapter 1. As Riley (1998: 29) notes, 'Changing lives ... are in continual interplay with changes in society and its structures. Neither can be understood conceptually without the other.' We have seen above that the temporal gaze may be directed forwards to the future, or backwards towards the past, or it may oscillate between the two. Similarly, in the micro–macro plane, the focus of the temporal lens can be adjusted to produce a close-up vision of individual lives, or a wide-angled view of social or historical processes. The micro–macro plane has been the focus of a burgeoning number of life course studies. Unfolding biographies have been explored in the context of a range of external landscapes, from shifting patterns of education and welfare provision, to forced resettlement and transformations in political structures (Pollard and Filer 1999; Patrick 2017; Scudder and Colson 2002; Holmberg 2012). As shown in Chapter 1, it was Mills (1959) who first provided the impetus for temporal researchers to explore the interface between biography and history. However, he had little to say about how such a task might be accomplished, leaving successive generations of researchers to grapple with this problem (Giele and Elder 1998: 7; Shanahan and Macmillan 2008: xii).

A useful starting point here is the recognition that biography and history are not discrete domains that can be viewed dualistically. They are part of a continuum of dynamic processes, within which lies the meso domain of collective lives (families, organizations, communities, generations, institutions etc.). The meso domain, the world of shifting social relationships and structures, plays a crucial role in mediating between biography and history (Riley 1998: 45). Nor is it simply located between micro and macro, for it constitutes an interlocking and inter-dependent 'level' of social experience and practice (Riley 1998: 45). Nielsen (2003: 1–2) describes this as a subtle and ongoing interaction that produces societal change through a process akin to osmosis. In like vein, Bronfenbrenner's (1993) ecological model of human development comprises five interlocking domains of influence that span the micro–macro plane. These are micro systems; meso systems; exo systems (in which at least one linkage in the chain has an indirect influence on the original person, for example the impact of employment on parents, and hence on their children); macro systems; and chrono systems. The last is an 'umbrella' temporal domain that denotes change or continuity in the broader social environment. In Bronfenbrenner's view, these varied domains are nested inside one another, like Russian dolls, and he proposes that research designs should investigate their simultaneous connections (1993: 38).

Bronfenbrenner's framework has been utilized in a variety of policy contexts where there is a need to understand how individual, interpersonal and institutional spheres of life influence each other over time, and to what extent lived experiences mesh with policy processes (Molloy and Woodfield with Bacon 2002; Lewis 2007). Temporal researchers who work across this plane frame their enquiries in a variety of ways, exploring, for example, the intersection of individual, family and industrial time (Hareven 1982), or biographical, generational and historical time (Neale, Henwood and Holland 2012; Holland and Edwards 2014). Broadly similar schemas underpin large-scale longitudinal studies, this time couched in the quantitative language of age effects (biographical processes), cohort effects (collective processes across a cohort) and period effects (broad historical processes). Elder's comprehensive life course paradigm (1994; Elder and Giele 2009) follows a similar pattern, spanning the agency of individuals, linked lives or social ties to others and historical and geographical location.

Re-focusing the temporal lens still further permits a close-up view of these micro–macro domains, and reveals further flows of time embedded within them. In the micro domain, for example, it is possible to discern both 'inner' and 'outer' constructions of biography, the former permitting insights into the psycho-social dynamics of identity and the place of emotions in the construction of psycho-biographies (Nielsen 2003; Thomson 2010a, 2012; Du Plessis 2017). Drawing on the work of Chodorow, Nielsen (2003: 1–2) suggests that an individual's psychological make up, the formation of subjectivities and motivations, can be seen as historical phenomena, inviting exploration of the inter-dependent dynamics between emotional realities, cultural constructions and historical context, in short, between self and society (Neilsen 2003).

Similarly, the meso domain encompasses collectives of different scales, from small-scale family, friendship or interest groups, to larger institutional structures, to the complex machineries of government. It is in this domain that social structural configurations shape and re-shape human relations of care, support, dependency, solidarity, division, power and inequality. Finally, in the historical domain, transformations in society are evident at both local and global levels. The tempo of such changes may range from abrupt 'watershed' moments (the fall of the Berlin wall), to incremental processes such as the evolving place of women in the labour market, or the gradual shift from religious to secular society (Miller 2000).

While the value of working across the micro–macro plane is beyond doubt, it can create challenges for researchers. Methodologically, building macro-historical time into QL studies that have a limited longitudinal reach requires creative approaches to design, sampling and data generation, as the chapters below will illustrate. A more pressing and seemingly intractable issue concerns the theoretical challenge of teasing out micro–meso–macro influences and discerning their relative salience in how lives unfold. This raises doubts about the feasibility of disentangling, let alone explaining the multiple factors across the micro–macro plane that shape and transform lives (Giele and Elder 1998; Elliott 2005: 110–11; Brannen 2006: 150). Working round this problem requires a shift in focus. Rather than seeking unitary or definitive causal explanations, it may be more productive to aim for theoretically driven, 'plausible accounts' of the constellation of social mechanisms and historical processes through which life course changes occur (for an example, see Winterton and Irwin 2012). It is worth recognizing, too, that since these accounts are socially and spatially situated and generated at particular moments in history, they are context dependent and their meaning is inherently provisional (Elliott 2005: 111).

## Time–space: The spatial dimensions of time

This plane reflects the 'when' and 'where' of time: the intrinsic connections between time and space as a means to locate and grasp the meaning and significance of events and experiences. While clock time is spatially adrift, abstract and 'empty', fluid time is grounded in real-world events and practices. It emerges within and is made tangible through the varied spatial settings of people's lives, which may be distinctive in terms of geography, topography, culture, language and so on. May and Thrift (2001: 3) observe that multiple, dynamic time, 'is irrevocably bound up with the spatial constitution of society (and vice versa)'. Indeed, space and place are central to our understanding of the unfolding life course. The cultural environments into which people are born and grow up (from ghettos to leafy suburbs) exert a powerful influence on their sense of self, and how they position themselves in relation to others (Compton-Lilly 2017). At the same time, a simple change of locality may be instrumental in enabling people to establish new patterns of living, forge new identities or escape old ones (Elder 1994; Laub and Sampson 1998).

Working across this plane has produced some pioneering lines of enquiry in recent years, described variously as geo-dynamic or geo-biographical research, or latitudinal or transnational ethnography (Barnard 2012; Falola 2015; Schmidt-Thome 2015; Lee 2015). Taking a 'latitudinal' approach, Barnard (2012) broadened his longitudinal ethnography of the Naro peoples of Botswana to include related hunter-gatherer groups living in multiple sites across the southern states of Africa. The spatial comparisons enabled him to discern more clearly the historical forces involved in changing hunter-gatherer culture (see also Howell 2012). As a further example, Lee (2015) traced the journeys of young Korean immigrants from New Zealand, where they had spent most of their childhoods, back to their homeland. She then followed up those who subsequently returned to their host country. By using a mixture of prospective tracking, ethnographic techniques and life history interviewing, she was able to shed light on how transnational identities and a sense of belonging are forged for those whose lives straddle two cultures.

Locating particular places in time makes it possible to discern how time is etched upon a landscape. This may occur at intensive as well as extensive tempos. For example, in his geo-temporal study of how local cityscapes are transformed from day-time to night-time, Back (2007) explores the tangible impacts that this transformation has for local residents and their sense of security, protection, power and danger. In this study, temporal variations through the course of a day create different experiences of space. But spatial variations may also create different experiences of time (May and Thrift 2001: 3; Chaplin 2002). Shaw (2001), for example, using accounts from the Mass Observation Archive and other documentary sources, investigated how the intensity and pace of social time varies across cultures, and across different spaces within cultures (urban/rural, industrial city/small town life). She found significant variations in the amount of time allotted for work, rest, meals and other tasks of daily living. Time keeping also varies, in some cultures (such as Germany) driven by a rigid adherence to clock and calendar, and in others (Finland, Brazil and large parts of the global South) exhibiting a more unhurried approach, where people gather over hours or even days. Time in these slower places is more elastic and forgiving; 'finding time' to oneself, or simply 'being' as opposed to always 'doing', is more highly valued. While time–space is pervasive in life experiences and processes, it offers particular scope for the investigation of geo-biographies, temporal geographies, migrations and resettlement, and for the study of 'liminal' (betwixt and between) spaces that create a different quality of time (Zerubavel 1981; Hockey and James 2003).

## Continuous–discontinuous: The synchronicities of time

This plane of time was first identified by Aristotle as a central component of his distinction between *chronos* (fixed) and *kairos* (fluid) time (Bastian 2014). Synchronicities cut across all the flows of time outlined above, raising questions about how individuals oscillate between past, present and future, personal and social time, biographical, generational and historical time, short and longer-term time horizons, faster and slower paces of existence and between biographical continuities and change. In short, we can consider here how people balance, reconcile or synchronize these different temporalities. There are many ways of exploring these temporal oscillations. In his large-scale longitudinal research, for example, Elder (1974) explored the impact of an adverse historical event (the Great Depression in the 1930s) on the life chances of varied groups of children. He found that those who lived through the Depression during their teenage years were more resilient than those who experienced this event as young, dependent children. Their radically different experiences were due, at least in part, to the differential timing of this historical event in their unfolding lives. Elder's findings sparked a widespread interest in how historical events are synchronized with life course processes.

On a smaller canvas, researchers have explored the timing of life course events within individual biographies. The timing of a transition into parenthood, for example, may be a challenge for those who do not conform to dominant perceptions of an appropriate age to have a child (Shirani and Henwood 2011; Neale 2016). Similarly, the discontinuities that may arise between individual lives and 'mainstream' practices and experiences has yielded an enduring interest in how people re-align or reconcile their values, narratives and practices over time. For example, studies of people involved in crime or addiction, or otherwise leading stigmatized lives, have explored how they oscillate between sub-cultural and dominant values and practices. Interesting insights have emerged about how people manage or reconcile lives that may be at variance with orthodox pathways and practices, and what factors may lead them from one to the other (see, for example, the case study of a prostitute in Plumridge and Thomson 2003; and Lopez-Aguado's 2012 study of a street-gang intervention programme).

Discontinuities between personal lives and the mainstream can occur in a rich variety of ways, for example, through changes in working environments, migration, transitions into parenthood, retirement or unemployment. Changing tempos can lead to a sense of dislocation as people find themselves marching at an unfamiliar, hurried pace, or languishing in a world that feels too unstructured for comfort (Shaw 2001, May and Thrift 2001). Living 'out of time' may be a temporary state, and as 'time out' from a pressured or challenging life it may be highly valued (see Baraitser's (2013) exploration of family 'mush' time). But where it is associated with unplanned or unwanted transitions that become entrenched, it can have a significant impact on life trajectories and on future health and well-being.

For those undergoing challenging biographical disruptions (bereavement, illness, job loss, forced migration etc.), time may seem to shrink, creating a sense of disorientation or dislocation from the mainstream, such that the seamless flow of life from past to future is disrupted (Bury 1982, Lovgren, Hamberg and Tishelman 2010). People commonly talk of 'taking each day as it comes' or 'living in the moment'. Living 'out of time' means shortened time horizons, a sense of time as fleeting or ephemeral, which can make future planning impossible and lead to risky practices. In their QL study of the financial implications of poverty, for example, Dearden and colleagues (2010) found that people acted rashly in running up huge debts. The overriding preoccupation with survival in the here-and-now led to a loss of care and concern for the past (burning bridges), and for the future (risky behaviour, a lack of aspiration, the loss of hope). This is the sense of liminality (time-out-of-time, betwixt and between) documented by Van Gennep (1960 [1909]) in his study of the rites of passage. The concept of liminality has been utilized in a wide range of contemporary studies to make sense of social processes such as chronic or terminal illness, poverty, 'doing time' in prison, transitional states, forced relocation and homelessness (see, for example, Kelly 2008; Neumann 2012; Szakolczai 2012, Bryant 2016; Blows and colleagues 2012).

## Intersecting timescapes

The five planes of time outlined above form a provisional basis for discerning how theoretical understandings of time may feed into empirical investigation. These planes are clearly not discrete or stand-alone, for they intersect and flow into one another. Past, present and future, for example, can be understood at different scales of time (biographically or historically), in different spatial contexts, and through differential experiences of the tempo, pace and synchronicity of time. Endless possibilities exist to refine these planes, and to discern myriad connections across and beyond them. Adam (1990) reminds us that, in focusing on one dimension of time, we should not lose sight of the others; as parts of a larger whole, they are all implicated in how lives unfold.

## Time and the life course

As shown in Chapter 1, life course research is centrally concerned with the flow of human lives, the positions that people inhabit in the life span; their life chances and experiences relative to others; and the dynamics of these processes through the intertwining of biographical and historical time. The study of individual biographies or life journeys is a central component of life course research (Chamberlayne, Bornat and Wengraf 2000). The focus may be on the dynamics of specific 'phases' of the life course (e.g. youth, older life), or transitions between these phases, or from one status or circumstance to another (e.g. into and out of schooling, parenthood, employment, poverty, ill health or crime). The factors that shape life course transitions are important themes, along with the mechanisms that mark or trigger change. Longer-term trajectories are no less important: for example, the 'age' trajectory through childhood and adulthood into later life; the 'family' trajectory through partnering and parenting into grand parenting; or the 'work' trajectory through education and un/employment into retirement. The intertwining of these varied trajectories and how they influence each other is also a key site for investigation. It is through the long sweep of a life over decades that historical processes come more clearly into focus, and the cumulative influence of earlier life patterns on later life chances and experiences can be more fully investigated and understood (Elder 1974; Giele and Elder 1998).

Understanding the life course in terms of the flow of human lives brings to the fore another of its key features: it is essentially a dynamic process, bound up with flows of time. While time is deeply implicated in the way that the life course is understood and researched, relatively little attention has been given to its temporal dimensions. Indeed, much longitudinal and life course research is empirically driven and under theorized (Reiter, Rogge and Schoneck 2011). Yet the life course can be understood in both 'fixed' and 'fluid' ways: in other words, how the life course is perceived depends in large measure on how time itself is perceived. From the perspective of 'fixed' time, life is seen to unfold as a predictable passage through a number of predefined developmental stages relating to the institutions of family, schooling, employment, health and so on (Berthoud and Gershuny 2000). The course of a life is conceptualized as a socially defined and institutionally regulated sequence of transitions which are reinforced by normative expectations (Heinz 2009, 474, 9). Much like 'fixed' understandings of time, the life course is assumed to have a universal linearity and a seeming objectivity that places it 'outside' those whose lives are under study. It has been likened to an escalator that carries us along in a uniform direction (Glaser and Strauss 1971; Riley 1998).

The contrasting approach offers a malleable view of the life course, underpinned by a more grounded, fluid understanding of temporal processes. It rests on the premise that the life course is socially constructed through lived experiences, subjectivities and the agency and social interactions of individuals and groups (Harris 1987; Holstein and Gubrium 2000). While recognizing the structural opportunities and constraints within which all lives unfold, this approach foregrounds the variability of life journeys, and the many different ways in which these journeys are crafted by individuals across time and place. Social constructionists, from Van Gennep (1960 [1909]) onwards, have reflected this fluidity in their research (Neale 2015). Harris (1987: 27–8), for example, sees the life course as, 'the negotiation of a passage through an unpredictably changing environment'. Moreover, the life course itself is far from a fixed entity. As Hockey and James observe, 'we have to account for changes in the shape of the life course itself: it is not only individuals who change but the categories that they inhabit' (2003: 57). This fluidity provides a challenge to the idea of clearly separated life phases or stages, linked through a linear and orderly set of steps that occur at prescribed times (Bynner 2007, Grenier 2012, Woodman and Wyn 2013).

## Rethinking turning points, transitions and trajectories

Exactly how biographies are shaped, and what kind of causal mechanisms operate as part of these processes, are crucial questions for QL researchers and for life course research more generally. Turning points, transitions and trajectories, the conceptual building blocks for life course research, are vital tools in addressing these questions. A burgeoning literature has debated the meaning and definition of these concepts (Hackstaff, Kupferberg and Negroni 2012), although, interestingly, relatively few accounts link these constructs or seek to discern their intersections. The discussion below seeks to clarify the interlocking nature of these building blocks, and bring to the fore their fluid, processual character.

### Turning points (trigger points)

The notion of a turning point is used here as a loose umbrella term to capture the plethora of critical events, defining moments, interactions or epiphanies that can act as mechanisms or triggers of change (Kupferberg 2012: 227). The rich metaphors used to describe these phenomena reflect subtle differences in their nature, suggesting the need to use these concepts with care (Clausen 1995; 1998; Carlsson 2012). A finely grained, qualitative lens is needed to discern these processes, which perhaps explains why they are often omitted in accounts that are concerned with wider structural processes of change (Wingens and Reiter 2011).

As the name implies, turning points are often viewed in instrumental and linear terms to mean a concrete change from one state to another. Elder (1985: 35), for example, suggests that they 'redirect paths'; more recently, they have been described as *fateful or critical moments* – points in the life course that are 'highly consequential for a person's destiny' (Giddens 1991: 112; Thomson and colleagues 2002; Holland and Thomson 2009). Certainly, these phenomena may be bound up with critical life events or experiences, turning points in the literal sense, for example, at the moment of a birth or death. Conversely, they may be artfully constructed, socially prescribed and carefully planned, for example, the ritualized entry into marriage, or the marking of a change in status, such as the awarding of a degree. Such events are instrumental through their expressiveness, combining core 'speech acts' with powerful symbolic representations that place people at the fulcrum of change. The idea that turning points have instrumental efficacy, involving a concrete change in the direction of individual or collective lives, is pervasive in the literature. It is for this reason, perhaps, that they are often subsumed within the broader category of transitions. Yet this tends to obscure their distinctive nature and their potential significance as causal mechanisms.

An alternative and less instrumental understanding of these phenomena stresses their subjective, fluid nature and their subtle influence through the flows of time. First, and perhaps most evidently, turning points are triggered in discrete and often striking moments in time. They have a fleeting quality. Their power lies in their propensity to create or instil changes in an *inner biographical disposition*, a process in which individuals or collectives take stock of their circumstances, assess this reality, understand it anew, and conjure a new imaginary future (Strauss 1997 [1959]; Hareven and Masaoka 1988; Clausen 1998). Howell (2012) for example, documents how an Indonesian community, the Chewong, arrived at a rapid rethink in their core beliefs about the status of Rattan, a sacred forest plant, which then enabled them to take advantage of new and lucrative opportunities to harvest the plant and use it for trade. While these arresting moments in time do not constitute life change in themselves, they are the potential agents or triggers of change (and for this reason, it may be more fitting to describe them as trigger points rather than turning points). They are also simultaneously forward and backward facing, the lynchpins for bridging continuities and discontinuities and marking and creating boundaries between past and future (Clausen 1995; Abbott 2001; Kupferberg 2012; Carlsson 2012). By their very nature, then, turning points occur in the moment, crystallizing elements of past and present circumstances, changing perceptions, identities and understandings, and opening up the possibility of an alternative pathway for the future.

This brings us to a second feature of these phenomena. Since they occur in the moment, their longer-term causal efficacy can only be determined through a backward gaze (Hareven and Masaoka 1988; Abbott 2001). While trigger points may have significant power at the moment in which they occur, their effects may be short lived. The subjective significance and meaning attached to a particular trigger point may shift over time, with some assuming enduring causal power, while others fade into insignificance (Plumridge and Thomson 2003; Holland and Thomson 2009; Jost 2012). They are best perceived, then, as subjectively defined phenomena, inhering in particular narratives of change, constructed with hindsight and, therefore, identifiable only in retrospect (Strauss 1997 [1959]; Denzin 1989, Clausen 1998; Abbott, 2001, George 2009).

This way of understanding turning points represents a challenge to the idea that one single, discrete event, experience or epiphany has sufficient causal power to bring about another event, or to effect a concrete change in the direction of a life or, indeed, that individual agency alone can bring about such changes (Carlsson 2012: 4). In other words, if turning points have any causal efficacy, what is likely to make a difference is their cumulative impact and how, in combination, they are situated and understood in particular contexts of change. Unlike fixed, instrumental entities, trigger points may accumulate in varied ways: as incremental nudges, or 'rehearsals' along a pathway (Thomson and colleagues 2002, Holland and Thomson 2009; Negroni 2012); as 'eddies' or 'drifts' or zigzag pathways in varied, sometimes random, and sometime conflicting directions (the forces of push and pull, to and fro, as people try out new paths and revert back to old ones, Howell 2012). They are, indeed, subject to a host of intervening social, structural and historical circumstances that impact on future pathways (Carlsson 2012). Since they are embedded within broader time horizons, the transitions and trajectories that make up the life span, they are not free floating and do not operate in isolation; they are part of the interplay between individuals and the social worlds they inhabit (Carlsson 2012). Overall, then, turning points operate at the crucial nexus between social structures and personal and collective agency (Kupferberg 2012: 227).

## Transitions and trajectories

Transitions are dynamic periods of the life course that constitute a passage from one concrete status or circumstance to another (Miller 2007; Shanahan and Macmillan 2008). They may unfold over varied periods of time, at different paces and intensities, sometimes occurring almost imperceptibly through a mixture of biological, biographical, collective and historical change. They also vary in the extent to which they are planned, prescribed, managed or desired by those involved. They may take the form of a series of mini transitions, marked by key milestones and prompted by a series of trigger point along the way. For example, the processes leading to and following a birth, death or chronic illness, or the preparations leading to a marriage and its aftermath, are all transitional periods marked by an accumulation of trigger points which, taken together, provide the momentum for change.

Transitions, in turn, are embedded within longer-term trajectories, the longer sweep of a life across the life span. These longer spans of time are marked by periods of continuity and steady states, as well as change. They are what Abbott (2001) calls 'master narratives', and they are influenced by a host of intervening factors across the micro–macro plane (Clausen 1998). Over time, it is possible to discern how varied trajectories intersect to create a unique biography; to explore how they are shaped through particular circumstances (e.g. 'upward' or 'downward' paths through privilege or poverty); or how they may unfold differentially (converging or diverging) for those with shared beginnings (Laub and Sampson 2003). Among many fruitful lines of enquiry are those that explore how, or whether, a particular transition (e.g. an early entry into parenthood) impacts on an overall trajectory (e.g. the broader socio-economic fortunes and life chances of young parents, Neale and Davies 2016). Over the longer term, too, the impact of external forces and the twin processes of continuity and change, stability and volatility on emerging trajectories are more clearly discernible, giving a particular pattern and shape to unfolding lives (Clausen 1998). Abbott (2001) reminds us that trajectories have an inertial quality: they are marked as much by stasis as change: enduring states, recurring patterns and structural equilibrium that may well overwrite, absorb or iron out the ripples of transitions and turning points.

Seen as interlocking processes, trigger points, transitions and trajectories share some of the characteristics of Bronfenbrenner's ecological domains of influence (see the micro–macro plane, above). They, too, are nested inside one another, like Russian dolls, but, in this case, operating across different horizons of time. It is the dynamic interdependence of these temporal processes that is the source of their meaning (Shanahan and Macmillan 2008). This suggests the need to take all three into account in exploring how dynamic processes unfold.

## Concluding reflections

This chapter has explored the conceptual underpinnings for QL research, stressing, in particular, the fluid, processual nature of time and the life course, and the interlocking horizons of turning points, transitions and trajectories. Thinking through these concepts is a foundational part of the design and development of a QL study. In order to support this process, five timescapes or planes of time have been outlined above, along with some pointers for how these might be used as topics of enquiry. Overall, the chapter illustrates the fundamental importance of engaging with time in the design and conduct of a QL study. Taking time into account is crucial, yet how time is understood, its nature and parameters, is no less so. Our vision will be impoverished if we focus solely on the clock and calendar. QL research has the capacity to bring lived experiences and flows of time into a common frame of reference, and to provide a bridge between sociological theories of time and more empirically-based life course and longitudinal studies. Adam (1990) observes that seeing things through the lens of time changes simply everything. In like vein, this chapter suggests that seeing things *qualitatively* through the lens of time produces a richness of understanding that can transform our vision of the social world.

# 3 Crafting qualitative longitudinal research: Design and sampling

Building on the conceptual foundations for QL research set out in Chapter 2, our discussion now turns to research design and practice. The focus here is on the temporal logic of QL research rather than its qualitative components.[1] Every dimension of the process is temporally fashioned and informed, from the construction of research questions and the longitudinal frame for a study, to issues of sampling, ethics, data generation and analysis. The aim in this chapter is to illustrate how the key dimensions of time introduced in Chapter 1 feed into design and sampling decisions.

The title of this chapter points to an important feature of QL research: it is as much a craft involving skill, dexterity and imaginative artistry as a rigorous social scientific enterprise (Mills 1959, Pettigrew 1995, Back 2007). In other words, it is a creative rather than a prescriptive process, offering endless scope for variations in design and innovation in the research process. The craft involves choosing the right design features and tools of investigation, and honing them for the enquiry at hand to maximize their descriptive and explanatory potential. The longitudinal frame for a QL study significantly increases the scope to combine varied research strategies and tools. As shown in Chapter 1, QL researchers are not wedded to one unitary approach; they are able to draw from a repertoire of approaches and blend them to produce a unique, tailor-made study (Saldana 2002). It is important to note that the creativity of QL research does not detract from

[1] There is a large literature on qualitative research design, although few general texts give more than cursory attention to QL enquiry. Ritchie and Lewis (2003) and Ritchie and colleagues (2014) are important exceptions.

the rigour that is needed to ensure a high quality study. On the contrary, it is an important dimension of methodological rigour, ensuring that a study is in tune with and able to reflect dynamic, real-world processes.

## The research process as a journey

All qualitative research is dynamic (Ritchie and Lewis 2003) but for QL research this is heightened in a number of ways. Firstly, key elements of research practice (sampling, recruitment, ethics, data generation and analysis) are not discrete, one-off tasks, but recur in cycles that are tied to each visit to the field. The engagement with time at the heart of QL research is mirrored in the research process itself: both can be conceived as journeys through time (Saldana 2003; McLeod and Thomson 2009). Secondly, changing perceptions of research settings and participants, new methodological and theoretical insights and developments in the researchers' personal and collective circumstances are all likely to influence the research journey. It is for this reason that QL researchers need to be reflexive about their shifting interpretations and practices and document these as the research progresses (Ottenberg 1990; Wallace and colleagues 1998; Filer with Pollard 1998; McLeod 2003). Thirdly, working through time means that the vantage point from which researchers and participants look backwards and forwards is continually shifting (Krings and colleagues 2012). Future time at the start of the study may well have become past time by the conclusion, requiring a continual switching of the temporal gaze. Through these shifting processes, QL researchers become 'time travellers' (McLeod and Thomson 2009).

The cyclical nature of the research process increases the scope for reviewing and refining research questions, themes, samples, fieldwork methods, ethical strategies and analytical insights as a study progresses. This continual openness to creative refinement is part of the rigour of QL research. It gives the necessary flexibility needed to respond to situations of flux and change and 'allows the unexpected to reconfigure the research' as it progresses (Grandia 2015: 312; Wallace and colleagues 1998: 79). As Scudder and Colson (2002: 206) observe, 'unexpected events bedevil the planning of long-term research. ... [A] rigid research design becomes a handicap over time.' But this flexibility also creates some challenges. It adds to the intellectual demands of the process and has resource implications for the timetabling and execution of a study. Moreover, it can engender a sense of adventurous pioneering and uncertainty in equal measure. As Saldana wryly observes, the process can take on the mammoth proportions and meanderings of Odysseus's journey to Ithaca:

> Imagine you're describing a road trip you took across Arizona, a trip where your journey was determined by careful planning ('After spending two days at the Grand Canyon, I was going to drive to Flagstaff'); unexpected opportunities ('But I discovered there was to be a pow wow in Chinle, so I drove there instead'); uncontrollable forces ('The heavy snowfall closed the highway and delayed me'); detours ('I took a state road instead of the highway because of construction and drove to Jerome'); and revised plans ('When I saw the Red Mountains of Sedona I just had to drive off the interstate for a closer look'). Such is the researcher's journey through a longitudinal qualitative study. (Saldana 2003: 15)

The danger in working with this degree of flexibility and contingency is that researchers may begin to lose track of what their research is about (Saldana 2003: 31). It is all too easy for the original focus to unravel when dealing with nebulous temporal processes that flow into each other, for this creates the temptation to discern change and flux everywhere. Maintaining some clarity concerning *what* it is that people are being tracked through (alongside who is being tracked, and how and why) will help to overcome this difficulty. In other words, it helps to be clear at the planning stage about research aims, questions and strategies, and to review, take stock and re-focus at critical junctures in the research process (Saldana 2003).

## Research questions and conceptual mapping

Developing a clear set of research questions at the outset can greatly help to navigate the research journey. These need to be qualitatively pertinent (Ritchie and Lewis 2003), for example, asking *how, why and where*. But they need to be framed in dynamic ways, posing questions, for example, about how temporal processes unfold; the nature, causes and consequences of change; and/or the influence of earlier events on later experiences and circumstances. Other temporal planes outlined in Chapter 2 (e.g. micro–macro or time–space) may also be interwoven here as appropriate. The *Following Young Fathers Study*, for example, sought to address the following dynamic research questions (Neale and colleagues 2015):

- How and why do young men enter into early parenthood? How is young fatherhood constituted, practised and understood in varied socio-economic and personal circumstances?
- How is young fatherhood 'worked out' over time? What factors shape the parenting experiences of young fathers and what helps or hinders their aspirations as parents?

Once drafted, the guiding research questions are not fixed; they are likely to be refined and polished iteratively as data are generated and the analysis unfolds. But they are an important starting point in establishing the parameters for a study. Devising a *conceptual road map*, a chart that sets out the guiding research questions and sub-questions, sources of data, field methods, and a list of themes that can feed into topic guides and broad-brush analytical codes will also help to guide the process. As a study progresses this map can be an invaluable aid in moving back and forth between theoretical premises and research practice.

## Designing QL research

Crafting a QL study involves working empirically with two planes of time that were first introduced in Chapter 1:

- Prospective–retrospective: looking forwards, looking back
- Intensive–extensive: time frames and tempos

The theoretical possibilities opened up by these planes were explored in Chapter 2; here we focus on how they feed into research design. The process involves a series of balancing acts across these two planes, as the discussion below will illustrate.

## Prospective–retrospective: Looking forwards, looking back

As indicated in Chapter 1, dynamic data can be generated in two broad ways: prospectively (looking forwards) or retrospectively (looking backwards). A *prospective* approach is the core design associated with longitudinal research, and the prime way to build cumulative knowledge about dynamic processes

(Howell and Talle 2012). People are followed in 'real time', capturing changes and continuities as they occur, and anticipating them in the future. This gives the research a forward momentum. Since revisits are anticipated, each new wave of fieldwork is shaped in relation to the previous waves, with the aim of building an emergent, dynamic picture. Ideally, prospective studies are planned from the outset, but in practice they are often created opportunistically by building on an earlier synchronic (snap-shot) study. Since all studies reflect the historical times in which they are located, the original study becomes an important baseline upon which to build cumulative insights.

A *retrospective* approach, on the other hand, is essentially historical in nature. It explores dynamic processes through hindsight, a gaze backwards in time from the vantage point of the present day (see Chapter 1). Quantitative researchers tend to regard retrospective approaches as 'quasi-longitudinal' on the grounds that they are unreliable. Since people's memories are said to be faulty, they 'telescope' events and facts either forwards or backwards in time, so that a clear and accurate chronology cannot be generated (Scott and Alwin 1998; Ruspini 2002). However, from a qualitative perspective, perceptions of the past are not fixed, and the search for some objective truth beyond the shifting interpretations and practices of the participants will always be elusive. In a QL context, the limitations of this approach reside rather more in the direction of the temporal gaze; on its own, looking backwards limits the ability to discern the drivers and impact of changes as they occur (Leonard-Barton 1995). Nevertheless, a retrospective approach offers a valuable means of reconstructing historical and biographical processes and discerning subjective causality, often over considerable periods of time (Scott and Alwin 1998). Studies that rely on retrospective methods alone are also relatively quick and cost effective (with all data generated through a single visit to the field). It is important to note, however, that prospective and retrospective orientations are not either/or modes of enquiry; they are complementary and are often productively combined (Scott and Alwin 1998). The most effective QL designs build retrospective elements into a prospective study, creatively blending them so that the temporal gaze oscillates between past, present and future and explores their complex intersections.

## Intensive–extensive: Time frames and tempos

We begin our discussion here with a consideration of the time frames and tempos of QL research, before going on to explore intensive and extensive designs. As shown in Chapter 1, the time frame for a QL study (the overall time span of enquiry) and its tempo (the number, spacing and continuity of visits to the field) are intertwined processes. Together they constitute the longitudinal frame for a study. Researchers who are new to QL research commonly ask how many waves of data are needed to qualify as a QL study, and over what time periods (Saldana 2003: 33). At a minimum, data need to be generated at two points in time to create the basis for temporal comparisons. However, there are no rigid prescriptions or easy answers to these questions. As shown above, these uncertainties reflect one of the challenges of QL research: it is always in danger of becoming unbounded, with never-ending possibilities for stretching backwards and forwards through time:

> When does a change process begin and end, especially where the unit of analysis is the continuous process in context? ... When does the fieldworker start and stop collecting data? Does one stop peeling the layers from the onion only when the vapours inhibit all further sight? There are, of course, no absolute and simple answers to such questions. (Pettigrew 1995: 98)

Time frames and tempos are usually shaped in relation to the research questions, the nature of the process under study, the characteristics of the sample, the practicalities of funding and the availability of resources. Two strategies are worth highlighting here:

- Clear baseline and closure points are needed to create the time frame for a study;
- Time frames and tempos should mirror the process under investigation.

These strategies ensure that there is a temporal logic to the research process. They are important means of anchoring a QL project in time, helping to delineate the overall duration of a study and, crucially, to contain it.

### Baselines and closure points

The baseline for a QL study might be defined as a point of change in the passage of time, a key historical moment, or a temporal marker of some kind, for example, the point at which people set up a new collective, become clients of a service, begin or complete a major transition, start a new phase of life, or face a significant change in the external landscape.

A baseline can be understood conceptually rather than as a discrete chronological moment (Lewis 2007). This allows for more than one baseline to be built in for different sub-samples, or to address different dimensions of the research questions (Lewis 2007). It may be determined biographically, in relation to the changing circumstances of individuals, or historically, in relation to changing external events, or both. Patrick (2017), for example, chose a change in UK welfare legislation as the baseline for her study of the lived experience of welfare reform. She traced the introduction and effects of the change on her panel of participants from the time the British Coalition Government came into power, through to the end of its term of office (2010–15). If the start of fieldwork does not coincide exactly with a baseline, a retrospective account can help to capture the event or moment. As far as possible, baselines and closure points should be driven by the temporal logic of a study, although in practice, both may have to be determined on pragmatic, resource-related grounds, tied to the period of funding.

### Mirroring the dynamic process

Applying the temporal logic of enquiry, QL researchers tend to fashion their studies in ways that 'fit' the dynamic process under investigation. For example, studies that track the clients of a service may tie the waves of fieldwork to the frequency and duration of contact between client and service provider. This was the case for Farrell and colleagues (2006) in their evaluation of New Labour's *Job Retention and Rehabilitation Pilot Scheme*. The study involved six months of fieldwork (six interviews, conducted at monthly intervals) with a panel of thirty-six people who had taken part in the scheme. The tempo for the research mirrored the tempo of the pilot scheme (cf. also Corden and Nice 2007). As a further example, studies of the transition to parenthood are typically built around a 'before and after' model, involving three waves of fieldwork over a twelve- to eighteen-month period (the early stages of the pregnancy, around the time of the birth, and some months after the birth, for example, Miller 2005; 2015).

### Flexible tempos

The mirroring process outlined above suggests the need for a flexible tempo that can be adjusted as a study unfolds. Indeed, whatever tempo is initially chosen, it may evolve over time in ways that are sensitive to the tenor of people's unfolding lives and responsive to changing conditions.

This is one of the ways in which QL research differs from large-scale quantitative studies, where participants are more likely to be followed at regular, predetermined intervals, spaced over years (Ruspini 2002: 4). Flexibility of follow-up can enable participants to engage in a study when they are able, or for researchers to respond to critical moments as they occur. Calman, Brunton and Molassiotis (2013), for example, report that a flexible tempo would have enabled them to follow their sample of terminally ill cancer patients on a case-by-case basis, mirroring how the disease progressed for each individual. Instead, their 'blanket' schedule meant that several participants declined rapidly and died before the researchers were able to revisit them.

A flexible tempo, tailored to the needs of individual participants, may also allow researchers to return to the field opportunistically, for example, to help sustain relationships or capture important historical moments as they occur or, more pragmatically, to respond to changing circumstances in the research team (Pollard 2007). Overall, the notion that time frames and tempos should be flexible in order to mirror the process under study can be very helpful, but it also needs to be tempered by resource and project management considerations. Too much flexibility may unravel a carefully specified study and confound pre-existing work schedules. Moreover, building in extra waves of fieldwork is expensive and time consuming, and adds to the complexity and magnitude of data generation and analysis. It is all too easy to be over-ambitious and underestimate the time needed between waves of fieldwork for rest, reflection, data management, cumulative analysis, and preparations for a return to the field. Nevertheless, building provision for some flexibility in the field at the project design stage can help to ensure a good fit between the tempo of the research and the tempo of the processes under study.

### Intensive–extensive designs

While there are as many time frames and tempos as there are QL studies, it is possible to identify a spectrum of approaches ranging from intensive to extensive designs. At one extreme, people may be traced *intensively* through particular transitions via frequent or continuous visits to the field. At its most intensive, QL research takes the form of ethnographic immersion. This affords a greater depth of engagement, yielding insights into the rhythms, tenor and synchronicities of daily lives, and the minutiae of change. In these contexts, rather than repeated *waves* of data generation, which imply periodicity, the process is more akin to a *stream* or *flow* of data and insights, which are gathered in 'drops or ripples' (Saldana 2003: 33). This brings to the fore the 'journey along with way' (Neale and Flowerdew 2003). Instead of making bald comparisons between two snap-shots in time, a more intensive approach generates a cyclical, reflexive and processual understanding, 'a description *through* time' (Howell and Talle 2012: 12, 17).

Intensive styles of research are likely to be conducted over relatively modest lengths of time (several months to several years), leading Saldana (2003: 35) to describe them as 'shortitudinal'. As well as being suited to the relatively modest funding streams that are currently available, they are ideal for tracking individuals through discrete transitions (e.g. the process of getting married, retiring from work, a hospital admission), or exploring a collective event or process (e.g. the birth of a new community initiative, or a time of national celebration or mourning). Intensive designs can also support the process of staying in touch with mobile or marginalized participants, and enable the production of findings for policy in the short to medium term (Molloy and Woodfield with Bacon 2002; Corden and Nice 2007).

In health, welfare and social care settings, a relatively intensive approach is commonly used to explore the introduction of new policy interventions and their short- to medium-term impact on service users. Harocopos and Dennis (2003), for example, tracked a sample of drug users intensively over eighteen months to investigate the effectiveness of a health intervention programme. The baseline for the research was the admission of the participants to a treatment and rehabilitation centre, where intensive ethnographic methods were used over several weeks to get to know and recruit the participants into the study. Thereafter participants were revisited at a less intensive and slowly diminishing tempo (five waves of interviews, conducted at one month, four months, eight months, thirteen months and eighteen months beyond their discharge from the unit).

At the other end of the spectrum, people may be traced more *extensively* through regular, occasional or 'punctuated' revisits to the field (Burawoy 2003). These visits may be spaced over many years or even decades. As indicated in Chapter 1, such extensive tempos are commonly found in large-scale longitudinal studies, the latter stages of longitudinal ethnographies and in sociological re-studies. The longitudinal frame here is akin to a series of synchronic snap-shots, or movie 'stills' gathered at discrete historical moments, while time becomes a linear 'stretch' between two or more points in time (Neale and Flowerdew 2003; Talle 2012). This is one of the ways in which QL researchers can engage with the micro–macro plane; the greater the historical distance between visits, the greater the likelihood of capturing broad transformations in the social fabric. In an extensive design, the distinct temporal boundary between field visits frees the researcher to look anew, with fresh eyes (Talle 2012). However, the time distance between visits diminishes the scope to discern the intricacies of dynamic processes and the ebbs, flows and detours that are continually occurring between the movie 'stills' (Neale and Flowerdew 2003). It also increases the challenge of maintaining a panel of participants; it may be necessary to retrace participants before they can be invited back into a study (see Chapter 4).

It is important to note here that intensive and extensive tempos and time frames are complementary. They form a spectrum of approaches that may be combined or which merge into each other at different points in the research process.[2] An intensive design, for example, may well evolve over time into a more extensive study or re-study, thereby capturing different flows of time. This is commonly the case for longitudinal ethnographies (Foster 1979; Gordon and Lahelma 2003; Talle 2012). It is also increasingly evident in interview-based studies. For example, working over very different time frames, Miller (2005, 2015, 2017) revisited a group of participants whom she had followed intensively through the transition into parenthood some eighteen years earlier. With follow-up funding she was able to build a longer view into her study, complementing the earlier three-wave prospective study with a retrospective reconstruction of the years of 'active' parenting for her sample (cf. also Furstenberg, Brooks-Gunn and Morgan 1987; and Laub and Sampson 2003). Overall, securing funding

---

[2] These different tempos have long been recognized by anthropologists. Firth (1959) distinguishes between *continuous diachronic* approaches and *dual synchronic* approaches; Foster and colleagues (1979: 9–10), between *continuous studies* and *re-studies*; and Howell and Talle (2012) between *multi-temporal* studies and *re-studies*. Similar distinctions are made by QL researchers (see Holland and colleagues 2006; and Warin 2011, who characterizes her fourteen-year study of school children as intermittent ethnography). Yet as Peterson Royce and Kemper (2002: xvi) observe, within the overall time spans allotted for longitudinal ethnography, there is 'considerable variation in length of time, in original impetus, in goals, in the time between field trips, and in the composition of research personnel'. These different tempos, then, do not represent discrete modes of longitudinal enquiry but are best understood as part of a spectrum of tempos that shade into one another.

for extensive research is likely to be a challenge for QL researchers. Most commonly, an extensive time frame evolves in piecemeal fashion through several phases of funding. But a far-sighted researcher will plan for a longer term revisit to the field and ensure, as far as possible, that samples can be maintained and data generated, documented and preserved in ways that facilitate this process.

## Temporal sampling: The logic of cases, themes and time

Qualitative sampling involves identifying an appropriate range of cases or units of study as the basis for empirical investigation and analysis (Ritchie and Lewis 2003). Choices need to be made about who (or what) to sample, how many cases to choose, what kind of variations to build in and when and where to sample them. These interlocking decisions constitute a sampling strategy. While samples may be drawn from a wide population of people, social events and so on, the main sampling units in a QL study are likely to be individuals or small collectives, alongside the networks, events or settings in which their lives are unfolding.

Adding time into a sampling strategy complicates the process, but also enriches it. Time has an impact on sample size, the breadth and depth of investigation, when to sample, what variations to build in, and how comparisons between cases are to be understood. A QL case is inherently dynamic and process driven. The units of study are likely to be identified not only through the varied characteristics of particular individuals or groups, or in different spatial contexts, but also in relation to temporal processes. In other words, key themes are investigated not only by sampling across cases but also by sampling through time. For example, in a longitudinal ethnography of children's school careers, set initially in one primary school, the units of study were the children, parents and teachers; the varied micro-settings of the children's lives (classroom, playground and home); and the seven school calendar years through which the children were being tracked (Pollard with Filer 1996; Pollard and Filer 1999). This became the conceptual framework for gathering, organizing and analysing data about the children's unfolding lives. Time itself became a unit of study, seen in relation to the biographies of the children and the varied micro-cultures and broader education structures that shaped and re-shaped their school careers. Overall, the logic of QL enquiry brings the complex relationship between *cases, themes and time* into a common conceptual framework. All three must be held in mind and attended to in the design and conduct of a study. This conceptual framework determines how cases in a study are constituted and how they are analysed (a theme explored further in Chapter 5).

## Purposive sampling

In the discussion below, the basics of purposive sampling and what this means for the size, breadth and depth of a QL sample are outlined. The parameters of temporal sampling are then considered, including the process of re-sampling over time and the nature and utility of longitudinal panels and cohorts. However the cases in a QL study are defined, the aim is to sample those that have explanatory power: that is, that will give insights into the study themes. Purposive sampling logic is commonly used to identify a range of cases that the researcher can then read across for the purposes of analysis. The aim may be to sample for typical, particular or extreme cases, or to work across a broad spectrum of circumstances and experiences, for example, along the axes of gender, age, ethnicity, socio-economic circumstances and/or geographical setting. Quotas for each sampling criterion (e.g. numbers in each age group) may be drawn up, using a matrix that guides the selection process (Ritchie and colleagues 2014).

## Sample size, breadth and depth

Purposive sampling has a theoretical logic that obviates the need for large or 'representative' samples. The emphasis is on understanding experiences across a range of complementary cases, rather than measuring similarities and differences across strictly comparable cases (Pawson 2006). The size, breadth and depth of a QL sample will vary from one project to the next, depending on the priority accorded to a *case-study* or *cross-case comparative approach*. Case-study approaches identify a relatively small number of cases, or even one distinctive case that can offer an in-depth, holistic understanding of social processes. Sampling across a small number of family groups or organizations, for example, offers scope for a detailed exploration and comparison of their varied pathways through time (Pettigrew 1995; Macmillan and colleagues 2011). This was the approach taken by Pollard with Filer (1996: 293) in the *Identity and Learning Programme*, a twelve-year longitudinal ethnography of children's journeys through the education system. The researchers had initially planned to sample children from two contrasting primary school settings. While they eventually achieved this goal (Pollard 2007, see below), at the outset, this plan had to be put on hold when anticipated funding did not materialize. Instead, an opportunity arose to work with a committed head teacher in one particular school. In a prime example of opportunistic sampling, the researchers adopted an ethnographic case-study approach and recruited ten children drawn from the same year group in this one school setting. Tracing the lives of these children through the varied micro-spatial and cultural settings of their lives (classroom, home and playground), against a backdrop of shifting educational policies and school practices, revealed subtle changes in their fledgling educational trajectories over the years of their primary education (Pollard with Filer 1996; Pollard and Filer 1999; Filer and Pollard 2000; and for a similar study see Gordon and Lahelma 2003).

Alternatively, building larger samples, with greater heterogeneity across ages, generations, settings, circumstances and/or life experiences, increases the scope for cross-case analysis. Multiple samples may also be drawn into a study to aid comparison across spatial settings, or to represent different stakeholders across the micro–macro plane (see Chapter 2). Qualitative Panel Studies (also known as QPS or QPR) are prime examples of 'scaled up' studies that work with relatively large and diverse samples. Burton, Purvin and Garrett-Peters (2009), for example, traced the lives of 256 low-income mothers in their six-year longitudinal ethnography, a study nested within a large-scale longitudinal survey of 2,402 families across three US cities (for a similar mixed-methods design in the context of global poverty research, see Morrow and Crivello 2015). Similarly, the *Welfare Conditionality Study* recruited 480 cases, representing nine sub-samples of welfare recipients, who were drawn from a range of localities across England and Scotland. The sample also included welfare providers, whose perspectives were sought in one-off interviews (www.welfareconditionality.ac.uk).

However, such large samples are unusual in the canon of QL studies. Whatever the balance between a case-based and cross-case comparative strategy, there is a clear trade-off between depth and breadth of investigation. Qualitative researchers in general try to keep samples sizes to manageable proportions (averaging around fifty cases), to ensure that the necessary depth of explanation is not compromised (Ritchie and colleagues 2014). For QL research, this becomes even more of an imperative. A proliferation of varied cases and settings and an accumulation of temporal data, often in quick succession through the cyclical waves of a study, can quickly become unmanageable. Researchers may find themselves grappling with, or sinking under the mammoth task of generating, re-generating, analysing and re-analysing an increasingly large and unwieldy dataset. Even the average sample sizes used in qualitative research (fifty cases) may become much less manageable when a sample is to be followed intensively over several waves of fieldwork, and where the drive is to build cumulative insights as a study progresses. The challenges may be all the greater for lone researchers or small teams with limited resources.

Whatever the attractions of 'scaling up' QL enquiry, depth of explanation and insight is a crucial feature of QL research and should not be compromised. In this context, the trade-off between the depth and breadth of a sample also means a trade-off between the size of a sample and the frequency and intensity with which people are followed up. In other words, the tempo of a study is an integral component of a sampling strategy. Since decisions about the nature and size of a QL sample will impact on the tempo of a study these need to be considered together, as integrated dimensions of QL design. For all these reasons, QL researchers working intensively within relatively modest time frames are likely to plan for detailed investigation across a relatively small number of cases.

## Re-sampling through time

In all qualitative research, sampling is a dynamic process. The criteria for inclusion may change or be refined as fieldwork progresses (Ritchie and Lewis 2003). This is evident, for example, in grounded theorizing, where researchers continue to refine their sampling strategy and recruit new cases until they have 'saturated' a particular theoretical category (Charmaz 2006).[3] However, in QL research the dynamics of sampling

---

[3] It is worth noting here that temporal sampling is underpinned by a different logic to that of grounded theorizing. In grounded theory, sampling involves an ongoing search for *new cases* that can shed fresh light on emerging theories. The process comes to an end when categories or themes are 'saturated' that is, when new cases no longer spark new theoretical insights (Charmaz 2006: 113). Yet time cannot be 'saturated' in this way. The aim, instead, is to sample the same cases at different times, to discern whether and how they may change. Temporal understandings are under continual construction and refinement, creating fresh insights for each case with each return visit to the field. For a further discussion of these differences in relation to data analysis, see Chapter 5.

are particularly pronounced. Units of study such as couples, families, households and organizations may well shrink or grow or otherwise change shape or composition as a study progresses. Similarly, individuals initially recruited because of the relevance of their life circumstances or personal characteristics may not fit these sampling criteria over time. In a QL study this creates opportunities to investigate the nature of these transformations as the research unfolds. But there is also increased scope to purposively re-sample over successive waves of fieldwork. Sampling itself becomes part of the research journey, requiring researchers to decide how to draw a baseline sample, how to follow up the baseline and whether to recruit new sub-samples at a later date.

Not all of the baseline sample will necessarily be tracked over time. It is common for larger samples to be recruited into a panel at the outset, but for carefully selected sub-samples to be singled out for more detailed attention or more intensive tracking as a study progresses. This is part of a broader ethnographic strategy known as a *funnel* approach, or *progressive focusing* (Agar 1980: 13; Pollard 2007). The chosen sub-samples are likely to offer greater insights into the themes of the study, for example, exemplifying those in stasis or undergoing further transitions, or with particularly distinctive or diverging trajectories. The full baseline sample may then be followed up with less intensity and/or frequency (e.g. interviewing via telephone or the internet rather than in person). This is one of the ways in which the balance between breadth and depth in a QL investigation can be maintained, ensuring breadth at the baseline, but depth at follow-up. It is a sampling strategy that can save on limited budgets, and may be particularly suitable for lone researchers or small teams with limited time and resources.

Alternatively, researchers may choose to boost a baseline sample at follow-up. As shown above, in the *Identities and Learning Programme*, Pollard and Filer (1996, 1999) started out with a sample of ten children drawn from one primary school. Some years later they were able to boost the sample when they were given access to a further ten children from a contrasting primary school (Filer and Pollard 2000). Most of the twenty children were followed into the years of their secondary education, a process that involved expanding the settings for the research from two primary schools to nine high schools (Pollard 2007). Similarly, in the *Following Young Fathers Study*, the original sample comprised a group of twelve low-income young fathers who were tracked intensively over three waves of interviews. This was an 'opportunistic' sample, recruited and revisited through the support of a particularly committed practice partner. For the second phase of funding, which followed on seamlessly from the first, the sample was boosted to thirty-one young men, including those from middle-income families, and those without specialist professional support. This gave greater insights into the varied socio-economic trajectories and support needs of the young men and how these impacted on their fatherhood journeys (Neale and colleagues 2015). Boosting the sample in this way enabled an incremental development of this study from its modest beginnings.

## Longitudinal panels and cohorts

The participants in a prospective longitudinal study are commonly described as a *panel*.[4] This implies an established group of participants, with a shared identity and the capacity for a sustained engagement with the research process. Using purposive sampling logic, a QL panel may be constructed in varied ways to enable comparisons through time. A common strategy is to build in one or more *cohorts*. These are individuals or groups whose fortunes are shaped by a shared experience, a common passage through the life course or a particular historical process, over *roughly the same period of time*. They are defined as 'aggregates of individuals who experience the same life event within the same time interval' (Ruspini 2002: 9). In other words, cohorts are anchored by shared experiences in time. This gives a great deal of flexibility in how cohorts are defined. They may be held together, for example, by their common age or generation, by a common life course experience (e.g. a concurrent migration, incarceration or retirement) or by a contemporaneous passage through an external landscape (becoming clients of a service, for example, or living through a change in policy, a war or a famine).

Perhaps the most well-known are the birth cohorts, samples born in the same year, who may be followed from birth or through a particular segment of the life course (Ruspini 2002). The times into which people are born are

---

[4] This terminology has its origins in quantitative longitudinal research, where it is associated with representative samples and a relatively long time frame. But it is also commonly employed in QL research, (see for example, Saldana 2003, Farrell and colleagues 2006, Krings, and colleagues 2013).

among the most powerful influences that shape who they are: 'To be young is to be young at a particular time and place: each age cohort is unique' (Colson 1984: 4). Sampling across one or more cohorts is a productive means of engaging with the micro–macro plane of time. Since cohorts are held together by shared experiences that occur contemporaneously, they can become lynchpins for discerning the links between biographical and historical processes of change. It is important to note that a cohort is by no means homogeneous: sampling across one particular cohort enables researchers to draw into a study those with different characteristics and living in varied circumstances. Laub and Sampson (2003), for example, explored the diverging trajectories of an age cohort of delinquent 'boys' over decades of change, uncovering the complex socio-economic, family and health factors that led some to persist with criminal careers and others to desist from crime.

### Sampling across cohorts

Sampling across different cohorts is a common strategy in longitudinal research, particularly in large-scale, extensive studies that seek to tease out how historical events are synchronized with life course processes (Giele and Elder 1998, and see Chapter 2). Drawing on longitudinal data from the long-running *Berkeley Guidance Study* and the *Oakland Growth Study*, Elder sampled two age cohorts of young people who were growing up at the time of the Great Depression (Elder 1974, Elder and Pellerin 1998; Shanahan and Macmillan 2008). The Oakland children experienced the Depression during their teenage years and were able to contribute to their family economies. The Berkeley children, who were eight years younger than the Oakland children, were small and dependent at the time of the Depression. As a consequence they placed extra strain on their family resources, resulting in adverse effects for them and their families. It was this strategy of sampling across two age cohorts that enabled Elder to discern the varied impact of a major historical event on people of different ages, and to produce new insights about the timing of historical events in people's lives.

Sampling across cohorts is also used in the more intensive designs of QL research. The strategy is most commonly employed in evaluation studies that seek to assess the delivery and effectiveness of social or health care programmes. By sampling two or more cohorts who may enter a programme sequentially, or at staggered (overlapping) times, it is possible to discern changes in programme delivery and how these impact on service users. For example, in their evaluation of the *Job Retention and Rehabilitation Pilot Scheme*, Farrell and colleagues (2006) interviewed three cohorts of service users (twelve cases in each). The study was conducted in three phases, each lasting six months and involving six waves of interviews. Each of these phases was devoted to a separate cohort of service users, whose experiences of the pilot were compared. In total, eighteen waves of fieldwork were conducted over an eighteen-month period, an intensive schedule that was facilitated by the small sample size.

A similar approach was taken in an evaluation of New Labour's *Pathway to Work Pilot Scheme* (Corden and Nice 2007), although here the cohorts of service users were staggered rather than sequential, and followed through overlapping time frames. The overall time frame was twenty-one months and involved nine waves of fieldwork, three for each cohort. This intensive design and sampling strategy yielded a relatively large sample size (over 100 people) and a steady stream of data and findings that were fed directly back into the development of the pilot scheme. Using staggered or successive cohorts within a QL panel design is a valuable means of exploring changes in individual experiences (the 'panel' elements), in relation to changes in service delivery (the 'cohort' elements). The approach is well suited to evaluation research, where a broader sample that offers greater scope for comparison may be needed, and where policy funders require quick results over the short to medium term (Corden and Nice 2007). However, as these researchers note, such sampling strategies can be complex to manage and involve particularly demanding schedules of fieldwork.

## Generational cohorts and family chains

Sampling within or across generational cohorts, or across inter-generational chains of family members, facilitates an exploration of the interplay between generational and historical processes of change. Generational cohorts are convoys of individual who are born and grow up within the same historical period. They are held together 'horizontally' through a shared cultural inheritance and contemporaneous experience of historical circumstances and transformations. When Mannheim (1952 [1927]) first identified generational cohorts, he stressed that they are not defined solely by age; indeed on this criterion alone generations would have no clear definition, given the seamless continuum of daily births and deaths. The temporal boundaries of a generational cohort are fluid and ill defined, and, unless those at the margins are 'sucked into the vortex of social change' (Mannheim 1952 ([1927]: 303), they may be inert, or passively orient themselves to those who are born either before or after them (Pilcher 1994; McLeod and Thomson 2009: 111). But the core members of a generational cohort will share a common sense of destiny that is forged through the shared times of their lives: historical, political and environmental processes, national events, technological advances, the rise of new cultural practices, shifting values and so on. Such processes may gradually coalesce to create a discernible shift in the social fabric, and the forging of a distinct generational identity (the 'war' generation, the post-war baby boomers, the millennial generation etc.).

Like all cohorts, generational cohorts are far from homogeneous in their life circumstances and experiences. They are likely to comprise varied sub-units that are defined along the axes of gender, class, ethnicity or community, and these too may develop distinctive identities that emerge in contrast or opposition to others (e.g. the 'mods' and 'rockers' of the post-war era). In *Growing Up Girl*, Walkerdine, Lucey and Melody (2001) followed the lives of a sample of young women from their early childhoods through to the cusp of maturity. The researchers used a multiple sampling strategy, drawing together cases that were being tracked prospectively; a second group, designed to boost the sample, who were interviewed retrospectively; and a third group who were sampled from an earlier study and the data re-purposed. The composite sample formed a classic generational cohort in the sense proposed by Mannheim. Of mixed class, ethnic and educational backgrounds, the young women were born within a decade of each other, and were forging their adult identities in a specific cultural milieu and at a time of structural inequalities and historical and social transformations leading up to the millennium (for a similar generational sampling strategy see Henderson and colleagues 2007).

### Sampling across generational cohorts and family chains

Drawing different generational cohorts into a study can serve two purposes. It affords access to the dynamics of inter-generational relationships and, depending on the number of generations included and how they are spaced, it can open a window onto broader historical processes of change. Bertaux and Delcroix (2000) suggest that a minimum of three generations is needed to create the necessary historical reach. In their study of disability across the life course, for example, Shah and Priestley (2011) sampled three generational cohorts of disabled people, those born in the 1940s, 1960s and 1980s. They were able to compare the experiences of each cohort as they grew up under very different regimes of health, educational and social care provision, and to chart changing experiences of disability that spanned half a century of change. This was a single-visit study that did not follow people through time. But the researchers were able to build a retrospective understanding of historical developments through this approach. Relatively few QL researchers have utilized this sampling strategy to date, although Hermanowicz (2016) provides a good example. He sampled three generational cohorts of academic science teachers (early career, mid-career and late career), basing his criteria on the year in which they received their doctorates. The fifty-five academics were drawn from different kinds of higher education institution in the United States. The longitudinal frame for this study was an extensive one, involving two waves of interviews separated by a decade. At follow-up, his sample of academics had moved into different stages of their careers (mid-career, late career and retired). At each wave, the researcher was able to explore generational and historical differences across the three cohorts. But the design also offered scope to explore the biographical transformations that had occurred for the sample as they moved from one generational position to another and, over a decade of change, to discern the institutional and social factors that had shaped their careers trajectories over time.

A related approach is to sample inter-generational chains of family members who are held together 'vertically' by their genealogical ties. This gives access to the inter-connecting lives, influences, legacies and internal dynamics of those who are linked through the bonds of kinship. Their unfolding trajectories are interlocking, with the fortunes of each generation (changes in relationships, employment, housing, health etc.) impacting on the lives of both older and younger generations in the chain (Elder 1985: 39). By working across a number of inter-generational family chains, insights also emerge into broader patterns of social change (Bertaux and Delcroix 2000: 71). An 'anchor' generation is usually identified for a study, from whom the chain can be built. It is worth noting that members of different family chains are not generational *cohorts* in the sense described above. They will not necessarily experience the same life events at the same historical time, for each family chain will have a unique historical range, depending on the ages of the generations, the spacing of their births and how many generations are sampled. Nevertheless, family chains are likely to offer valuable insights into macro-dynamic processes, alongside insights into the flow of family lives and influences across the generations.

To give one example, in a study of patterns of care within four-generation families (Brannen, Moss and Mooney 2004; Brannen 2006), the researchers sampled twelve inter-generational chains, each comprising between five and eight family members, giving a total of seventy-one family members in the study as a whole. The generational design gave significant historical reach to this study, from the 1930s Depression, to the post-war reconstruction and growth of the welfare state, to the neoliberal economic policies of the 1980s (Thatcherism). The researchers were able to explore how family support is shaped by life course position, family cultures and wider historical contexts.

Much like sampling across generational cohorts, sampling across family chains has been utilized, in the main, by researchers who wish to achieve historical depth retrospectively, through a single visit to the field (e.g. Bertaux and Delcroix 2000; Brannen, Moss and Mooney 2004; Brannen 2006). But there is ample scope to utilize this sampling strategy within a prospective QL design, as the following example shows. The *Making of Modern Motherhood Study* (Thomson and colleagues 2011; Thomson 2011) was designed around a critical moment of biographical and family change: the arrival of a new generation. Baseline interviews were conducted with a cohort of sixty-two women who were about to enter motherhood for the first time. Variations in age, social class, ethnicity, working status, living situation and proximity of family support were built into the baseline cohort. The age variation was particularly broad: the women were aged between fifteen and forty-eight at the time of their pregnancies. The researchers also sampled a variety of documentary sources that gave insights into popular cultures of motherhood at the time these women were giving birth, thereby situating the study in a particular socio-historical context.

For their follow-up interviews, the researchers funnelled in on twelve of the mothers from the baseline sample. These became the anchors for recruiting twelve inter-generational chains of family members into the study. These chains included grandparents, great grandparents and significant others. In a subsequent phase of the research, funded under the *Timescapes Study*, the researchers sampled six of these twelve chains, who were then followed up for two further waves of interviews. In this way, the researchers reconfigured their sample as the study progressed. While the number of family chains was too limited to permit an analysis of wider historical processes of change, the researchers were able to explore the 'gestalt' of modern day motherhood through the broad baseline sample, and develop insights into changing configurations of family relationships through the prospective inter-generational sample.

Overall, the examples given above demonstrate the flexibility and creativity of temporal sampling in QL research. Time clearly complicates the sampling process, but can also enrich it. Time influences the balance between depth and breadth of investigation and impacts on how and when variations may be built into a sample. It also shapes the way comparison and synthesis of evidence is to be understood (a theme developed further in Chapter 5). The facility to sample and re-sample though biographical, generational and historical time creates a wealth of flexible QL designs. It allows for different sub-samples to be followed over varied time frames and at different tempos. It offers scope to engage creatively with the micro–macro plane of time outlined in Chapter 2, to draw upon and read across data that is gathered prospectively or retrospectively, or that is generated for comparative breadth or case-study depth. Temporal sampling and re-sampling are complex processes that deserve careful thought and planning, for they are the crucial foundation upon which to build the generation and analysis of QL data.

## Concluding reflections

This chapter has given an overview of the craft of QL research, with a particular focus on design and sampling. The creativity and flexibility of this process has been stressed; for QL researchers this is part of the rigour needed to engage effectively with temporal processes. The research process itself becomes a journey that must be navigated and documented as a study unfolds. The overall process is guided through the construction of temporally-led research questions and a conceptual roadmap. Particular attention has been given to the temporal logic of QL design, including the balance between prospective and retrospective designs, and between intensive and extensive time frames and tempos. The value of a flexible tempo that mirrors the process under investigation has been explored, along with the need for clear baseline and closure points that can help to anchor and contain the scope of a study.

Sampling through time is underpinned by the temporal logic of working across cases, themes and time, and finding different ways to balance breadth and depth of investigation. The discussion has explored the basics of purposive sampling and what this means for the size, breadth and depth of a QL sample. The parameters of temporal sampling have been considered, including the process of purposively re-sampling over time to either 'grow' or 'condense' a study. Finally, the nature and utility of longitudinal panels and cohorts has been considered, and the potential to sample across generational cohorts or family chains has been explored. The importance of attending to these basic design and sampling issues, and thinking through their temporal dimensions is highlighted here, for they are the foundations upon which QL research practice is fashioned and refined over time.

# 4 Walking alongside: Sustaining ethical relationships

## Introduction

The 'real time' nature of QL research has been likened to the process of 'walking alongside' a panel of participants (Neale and Flowerdew 2003). The imagery of walking alongside has particular resonance in the context of longitudinal ethnography, where researchers are likely to accompany participants in the everyday settings of their lives (see, for example, Corsaro and Molinari 2000; Burton, Purvin and Garrett-Green 2009). This is walking alongside in a more literal sense, as 'fellow travellers' (Gordon and Lahelma 2003).[1] However, the imagery has resonance for QL research more generally, regardless of the intensity or continuity of field encounters. It is a useful metaphor for capturing the dynamic tempo of a QL study, its responsive and relational nature, and the central concern with how lives unfold through the stream of time (Neale and Flowerdew 2003). In reflecting the sensibilities at the heart of QL research, walking alongside also provides a welcome alternative to the notion of tracking people, which has instrumental (and possibly predatory) connotations. This chapter explores the intricate process of walking alongside a panel of participants. We begin by considering methodological strategies for recruiting a panel of participants into a QL study, and maintaining their involvement. The challenges of re-tracing participants whose whereabouts are unknown after a lapse of time are then explored. As the discussion develops, the ethical terrain within which these processes are embedded begins to

---

[1] This is also the case for walking methodologies in qualitative research. These are mobile, experiential data gathering techniques in which the researcher accompanies a participant through a particular setting or landscape of their lives, perhaps intensively over several hours, or more intermittently over a longer phase of field enquiry (Thomson 2012; Bates and Rhys-Taylor 2017).

emerge, culminating in a detailed consideration of the ethics of sustaining relationships in a QL study.

## Recruiting and maintaining samples over time

QL research relies on being able to recruit and maintain a panel of participants over time. The aim is to minimize sample attrition – the process whereby panel members drop out of a study. A refusal to participate or a failure to engage may occur for a variety of reasons, most of which are beyond the control of the researcher. Panel members may lose touch if their circumstances change, for example, through relocation, changing jobs, names or telephone numbers, breaking ties with family or social networks, or suffering illness or death (Farrall and colleagues 2016). In some cases, drop out is most evident where participants are undergoing particular difficulties in their lives (Harocopos and Dennis 2003). But it may also occur where people are doing better and opt to move on in their lives and leave the past behind them (Farrall and colleagues 2016).

In larger-scale longitudinal studies, there are varied views on what constitutes an acceptable attrition rate (ranging from 5 per cent to 30 per cent; Desmond and colleagues 1995). This has to be balanced against the duration of time over which a study runs. A 75 per cent retention rate over a twenty-year period is regarded as a significant achievement (Elliott, Holland and Thomson 2008). In small-scale, relatively short-term QL studies, however, the loss of even a few participants might represent a substantial proportion of the sample and materially alter the balance of experiences under investigation (Farrall and colleagues 2016). For example, assessing the impact of a health or social care intervention requires a panel with varied experiences of and responses to the provision. The loss of panel members may skew the sample towards either positive or negative experiences, creating a bias that can impact on the robustness of the evidence (Desmond and colleagues 1995; Harocopos and Dennis 2003). One way to compensate for this is to over-sample at the baseline, although this needs to be done with care to avoid overstretching the resources of the researchers (Calman, Brunton and Molassiotis 2013). The methodological challenges associated with maintaining and revisiting samples over time are common to all longitudinal research. Particular issues may arise where researchers are working with marginalized groups, or where the aim is to retrace a 'lost' sample after a lapse of some years (Dempster-McClain and Moen 1998; Laub and Sampson 2003; O'Connor and Goodwin 2012; Miller 2015; Farrall and colleagues 2016). A further complication arises where the unit of study is a family or organization, for this requires the sustaining of collective commitment and consent over time (Taylor 2015). Some of the strategies used by researchers to overcome these challenges are outlined below.

## Recruitment

Strategies for keeping in touch with participants need to be planned for and built into initial recruitment plans. Preparations for entering the field involve negotiating access to research settings and developing relationships with 'gatekeepers', as well as with potential participants. Recruitment traditionally occurs through leaflets and letters that describe the research. The process may be initiated via organizations or key workers who can broker the research with participants, or through more direct approaches (in person, by phone or via the web). As shown in Chapter 3, QL researchers may begin a study with a period of ethnographic engagement and/or set up focus groups as a precursor to in-depth interviews. These are effective ways to get to know participants, to develop trust and rapport and introduce them to a QL study before recruiting them into a panel. Such methods may also help to establish a sense of group identity and belonging to a study that can support the maintenance of a panel over time. However, recruitment into a longer-term study is not always straightforward. Recruiting family groups or organizations, for example, may take some time to negotiate with all those involved (Taylor 2015). Working with transient or marginalized groups, or in settings where verbal communication predominates, can also present challenges. In these circumstances it is worth seeking permission to keep in contact via a participant's social network: family members, friends, key workers and so on. A contact sheet can be set up to record participants' personal details (including full name and date of birth) and preferred means of contact, along with contact details for selected family members or friends (McNaughton 2008). This can be used to check and update contact details at each research encounter. Whatever the recruitment route, it is best to clarify the proposed time frames for the research, the longer-term commitment this requires and the likelihood that researchers will re-contact participants again in future. Attrition is less likely where participants are aware of the longer-term nature of the study and can make an informed choice (Desmond and colleagues 1995).

## Strategies for maintaining contact

A range of techniques may be employed to keep in touch with an existing sample. Posting letters or bulletins about the project, along with a greeting card, is a common tactic. This provides the foundation for following up informally with a text, phone call and/or house visit. Increasingly, researchers use web-based modes of communication (emails and social networking sites such as Facebook) for the same purpose. With their speed, ease and relatively low cost, these can be an invaluable means of working flexibly in the field, sustaining links with participants and containing the high costs of QL enquiry. Setting up a Facebook page for a project, or bringing people together in a group, can foster and help to sustain a sense of group identity and belonging among panel members.

However, strategies need to be tailored to the needs of participants. These standard techniques may not work where panel members are undergoing difficult transitions, or do not have stable homes or regular access to internet or mobile phone technology. In these circumstances, researchers often leave their contact details with participants, along with details of the next interview, and invite participants to get in touch whenever it suits them (Harocopos and Dennis 2003; Williamson and colleagues 2014). Setting up a drop-in centre that can be accessed by panel members when they wish is also worth considering. This might offer varied kinds of support or therapies alongside other incentives to keep people's interest or draw them back into a study (Conover and colleagues 1997). There are few limits on researcher inventiveness. Hagan and McCarthy (1997), for example, sought permission at the outset of their study to take photographs of the homeless men in their sample, and later used the photos to locate the men in their transient communities. Providing material rewards, particularly for low-income groups, can act as incentives to draw people into a study, at least in the early stages. Such payments may be regarded as a means to professionalize the relationship between researcher and participant (Harocopos and Dennis 2003). In recent studies, QL researchers have offered participants a £20 gift voucher for their time (£50 for a detailed life history interview or for keeping a daily diary), and provided other forms of in-kind support as appropriate, for example, meals, transport costs or taxis to travel to an interview (Bytheway 2012; Neale and colleagues 2015). Such provision needs to be factored into project budgets at the planning stage.

Building ethnographic elements into fieldwork can also be very effective in developing rapport, maintaining communications and sustaining relationships (Hemmerman 2010). This might include informal visits to the home of a participant or family member. Or it may involve attending events or visiting local settings where participants or members of their social networks may be found. In these circumstances there is a need to be flexible and 'field ready', in particular to be willing to conduct an interview at short notice or on the spot, rather than making a formal arrangement for a later date that may not materialize (Williamson and colleagues 2014). Conducting fieldwork intensively, with relatively frequent visits to the field, can facilitate the process of maintaining contact with marginalized groups or those with limited access to internet or mobile technologies (Dempster-McClain and Moen 1998; Calman, Brunton and Molassiotis 2013; Williamson and colleagues 2014).

### Working with gatekeepers and practitioners

Building and sustaining relationships with gatekeeper organizations or practice partners can be vital in maintaining a QL sample over time (Pollard with Filer 1996). However, a longer-term commitment from practitioners cannot necessarily be relied upon (Saldana 2003; Ward and Henderson 2003). The job mobility of professional workers and insecure, short-term funding in the public and voluntary sectors can also create constraints. A slow and painstaking process of nurturing working relationships with practitioners over months or years may be undone overnight. This then requires the researcher to switch settings, or start afresh with incoming staff who may have little interest in the research and no knowledge of the participants (Pollard with Filer 1996, Ward and Henderson 2003).

Where sustained professional support can be garnered, however, it can be of huge value. In the *Following Young Fathers Study* a specialist support worker became a practice partner in the project. He played a crucial role in helping to recruit a relatively nomadic and marginalized group of young men into the study, liaised between the researchers and the participants over the course of the study and ensured that the young men were able to participate (including, on occasion, finding them on the street and bringing them to interview) (Neale and colleagues 2015). In this case, the specialist remit of the practitioner gave him the time and resources to make these contributions. Clarifying the nature of the research and negotiating the longer-term commitment needed from the practitioner at the outset also helped. Attrition rates for panel members recruited through this particular route were very low compared to the rates for a subsequent sample of young men, who were recruited through a range of different agencies, and whose professional support was relatively fleeting and impersonal (Neale and colleagues 2015).

## Re-tracing participants over extensive time frames

Where there has been a significant lapse in time since a panel was last convened, or where the aim is to locate a sample from a legacy study carried out by earlier generations of researchers, panel members will need to be re-traced before they can be invited back into a study (Dempster-McClain and Moen 1998; O'Connor and Goodwin 2012; Miller 2015; Farrall and colleagues 2016). The practical strategies outlined above all come into play here, starting with writing to the last known address, or to named contacts, and following up with telephone calls and visits to field sites, where using personal contacts or simply 'asking around' can be very effective (Dempster-McClain and Moen 1998). But where these strategies fail, researchers can resort to a range of tracing techniques, based primarily on internet technologies and social media (Miller 2015; Farrall and colleagues 2016). Telephone directories and registers of voters are likely to be available on line (in the UK via www.192.com for the electoral roll). Google and Facebook searches can be conducted using people's names, occupations, leisure pursuits or interests; or searches can be made of company registers or the websites of particular organizations or community groups (Miller 2015, Farrall and colleagues 2016). Revisiting past interview transcripts can be helpful in identifying possible leads.

In tracing people from a legacy project that had been conducted forty years earlier, O'Connor and Goodwin (2010) had some success with personal contacts in the local community, and the now defunct *Friends Reunited* website. They also advertised their re-study in local print and news media to encourage people to come forward, although this indirect approach was less effective. Where such strategies fail, birth, marriage, death and obituary records may be checked (Farrall and colleagues 2016). Other potential sources are institutional or administrative records relating to the participants, for example, held by health, welfare, employment or educational agencies, churches or community groups, or the criminal justice system. Researchers report tracing over half of their original samples using these varied routes (Dempster-McClain and Moen 1998, Miller 2015; Farrall and colleagues 2016). Even after a lapse of forty years, O'Connor and Goodwin (2010), managed to trace 157 people from a sub-sample of 500 participants, resulting in 97 interviews. In this case, however, only ten of those interviewed were women, despite the efforts of the researchers to trace name changes through marriage registers. Tracing tools, then, can introduce further biases in a sample, but they are clearly effective in enabling researchers to extend the historical and biographical reach of an earlier study.

## When to give up?

The palette of techniques available to trace and maintain a QL sample over time, and the time, resources and stamina needed for these tasks may seem daunting. Farrall and colleagues (2016), for example, spent well over two years tracing and re-contacting a sample of 199 probationers before exhausting all possible leads. The process yielded a 50 per cent success rate. A pursuit such as this requires not only earmarked budgets but skilled, flexible and dedicated researchers who are well versed in longitudinal enquiry (Calman, Brunton and Molassiotis 2013; Williamson and colleagues 2014; Farrall and colleagues 2016). Indeed, the process of maintaining or resurrecting a QL sample can require the patience, ingenuity and tenacity that are commonly associated with private detection. Some researchers offer a 'finders fee' to practitioners and friends as an incentive to help, or resort to tracing agencies such as Equifax (Molloy and Woodfield with Bacon 2002; Dempster-McClain and Moen 1998), although, as Molloy and colleagues point out, such methods may breach confidentiality. Contract researchers may even be offered bonuses if they successfully retrace a sample (Bootsmiller and colleagues 1998).

Researchers often describe themselves as amateur sleuths when engaged in these activities (Warin 2011: 24; Miller 2015). However, this can be equated with the dubious practice of 'stalking', or coercion, implying that the researcher has turned predator. Not surprisingly, researchers may feel ambivalent about this, and, for the same reason, may eschew the very notion of 'tracking' participants, with its connotations of a power imbalance between the 'tracker' and the 'prey' (Williamson and colleagues 2014; Miller 2015). The language of 'revisiting' or 'walking alongside' is less contentious here. But these ethical concerns reinforce the principle that there have to be limits to how far researchers will pursue people, and the zeal with which they do so. In other words, the methodological drive to maintain or revitalize a sample has to be tempered with the ethical drive to respect people's privacy (an issue elaborated further below). For this reason, QL researchers commonly adhere to a standard rule of thumb: no more than two requests are usually made for a follow-up interview. The second request can clarify that no further contact will be made, but invite participants to get in touch if and when they could like to re-join a study at a later date (Farrall and colleagues 2016).

## Sustaining relationships

Whatever the ambivalences around these processes, and the significant commitment of time and resources that they take, it is re-assuring to know that most QL researchers report relatively low rates of attrition, even when working with marginalized groups such as drug users (Desmond and colleagues 1995). Sample maintenance is generally less of a problem in QL enquiry than in large-scale longitudinal research. This can be explained by the intrinsic nature of the research encounter. It is a sustained interpersonal process that seeks to understand people's lives and respect their world views. This means attending to the finer details of the encounter, for example, giving participants a choice over interview settings, modes of communication and who is present; and ensuring continuity of fieldworker wherever possible (or an effective overlap and handover where not). Overall, QL research transforms the task of *maintaining samples* into one of *sustaining relationships* (Neale 2013). Upholding the principles of compassion and respect for research participants may require researchers to recognize them as people first and participants second (Williamson and colleagues 2014: 82). In applying the ethics of care and respect in their study, Williamson and colleagues maintained an interest in the lives of the homeless women whom they encountered, and provided ongoing forms of emotional support for them that stretched beyond the time when the women dropped out of the research. In the event, the researchers were able to retain over 60 per cent of their sample over the course of a two year study.

Feedback from participants in QL studies reinforces the fundamental value of sustaining relationships as the key to maintaining a sample. Financial gain is much less often reported as an effective incentive. Farrall and colleagues (2016) found that when, in desperation, they offered an increased financial bonus to encourage people to re-enter their study this was markedly ineffective. Similarly, the homeless women interviewed by Williamson and colleagues reported that their initial financial motivation for taking part quickly gave way to more altruistic feelings, and the sense that they were privileged to be part of the panel (a sentiment that is often expressed among long-term research participants). A frequently reported motive for a continued engagement is the wish to give something back, and to help others in similar circumstances. Perhaps most significantly, the women interviewed by Williamson and colleagues (2014) reported an intrinsic satisfaction in being able to reflect on their journeys over time and share this with the researchers. Indeed, the commitment which participants develop to a QL study, alongside the sense of privilege and belonging that this can engender, can create challenges in bringing closure to the process (an issue considered below). In sum, whatever strategies are adopted to maintain a QL panel, the relational dimensions of the process are likely to be the crucial factors.

## The ethics of walking alongside

As the discussion above shows, ethical considerations are woven into the process of walking alongside a panel of participants.[2] The cardinal principles of research ethics are designed to ensure that participants are fully and transparently informed and participate freely in a study, that their confidentiality is protected, and that their dignity, autonomy and privacy are respected at all times (ESRC 2016). It is commonly held that QL research amplifies existing ethical considerations rather than raising new ones (McLeod and Thomson 2009: 76). Yet researching lives through time makes us sensitive to ethical issues and responsibilities in ways that

[2] The discussion here draws on Neale (2013).

are impossible to grasp through single-visit studies (Peterson Royce and Kemper 2002: xvi). For long-term ethnographers, these issues may extend to the changing role of the researcher in relation to the communities under study: from observer, to active partner, to advocate, with implications for researcher 'interference' in local systems of power and influence (Peterson Royce and Kemper 2002: xxx). More generally, the fluid and enduring nature of the research process opens up new dilemmas, and brings to the fore the transformative potential of well-established ethical principles. For participants, this applies to issues of consent as a process and the changing dynamics of research relationships. It also entails treading a careful path between reciprocity and professional boundary maintenance, and finding new ways to balance confidentiality, privacy, authenticity, protection and empowerment over time. As the discussion below will show, issues of consent, confidentiality and privacy all involve an ethical balancing act that becomes more pronounced as a study progresses.

Researching through time also opens up new ways to think about the relationship between proactive and reactive ethical strategies (Neale 2013). The first are procedural or advisory, constituted through ethical frameworks laid down by funding bodies and ethics committees, and through bodies of accumulated knowledge that researchers share to encourage good practice. The second are situated or emergent ethical practices that are context specific and based on a sensitive appraisal of local circumstances (Edwards and Mauthner 2002: 27; Guillemin and Gillam 2004; Warin 2011). Proactive and reactive strategies are broadly complementary, of course, and both are needed. But situated ethics has particular resonance for longitudinal enquiry, given the greater likelihood that unanticipated events, changing circumstances and fresh ethical dilemmas will emerge through time. As a study unfolds, researchers are likely to find themselves navigating through a changing ethical landscape. The needs and claims of individual panel members or different sub-samples will evolve over time and require flexible responses. Over time, too, a wider constituency of individuals and organizations (from researchers, institutions and data re-users, to family members and practitioners) may become implicated in the process. This requires new thinking about their varied needs and claims, albeit these are not of equal weight in ethical decision making. The prime 'stakeholders' in the research process, and the main focus of attention here, are the research participants themselves. In what follows, consideration is given to issues of informed consent, confidentiality, reciprocity, privacy, the extent of participation and the ethical closure of a project.

## Process consent

Informed consent in a QL study is an ongoing process rather than a one-off event (Saldana 2003: 24; Thomson and Holland 2003). Whether consent is sought in writing or is recorded verbally at the outset, this needs to be revisited over the course of the study, ideally at times when trust has developed. This may be done at each research encounter or through exploratory and flexible conversations that are held with participants at key intervals. Continuity of field researchers can be beneficial here in facilitating this process. Process consent creates some challenges: consent may be differently 'informed' when the future direction of a project may be flexible and subject to change, and a continual revisiting of consent may become a burden on participants and create instability. McLeod and Thomson (2009: 74) observe, too, that while participants may agree to each interview, they are unlikely to have a sense of the cumulative power of the data they are providing and what it may reveal about them over time.

As a study progresses care is needed to ensure that participants are free to choose whether or not to maintain their involvement. It is important that the relationship between researcher and participant does not become exploitative over time, as trust and familiarity grow, and that any subtle coercion to continue is avoided (Holland and colleagues 2006: 28). Where participants opt out, the flexible tempo of the research process is a real boon, giving people the option to re-join a study at a later date. This flexibility in the field seems to take the pressure off participants when the timing of fieldwork may not mesh well with changing circumstances in their lives. Where 'gatekeepers' such as family members or practitioners are involved in recruitment, or a study involves collectives of participants, care is needed to ensure that individuals are consenting freely and not being coerced into, or out of participation (Miller and Bell 2002; Warin 2011: 54-5). Deciding *how* consent is to be informed also requires consideration. Overall, it is good practice to be transparent from the outset about the objectives of the project, including the longer-term commitment needed from panel members; the steps taken to protect confidentiality; anticipated outcomes or impact; and plans for archiving and revisiting data. This includes the possibility that participants may be contacted after a lapse of time by existing or new research teams seeking to conduct a re-study. Finally, in some research settings it may be necessary to allay concerns about ulterior motives, and provide ongoing clarification and re-assurances about the purposes of a study. In particular (and regardless of the principle of reciprocity, discussed below), it may be necessary to clarify how social research differs in its aims and conduct from 'intervention' or 'support', and its limited capacity to effect desired changes in local communities (best framed as 'hoped for' rather than 'anticipated' outcomes; www. ethicsguidebook.ac.uk; Wiles 2013; Morrow 2013).

Similar considerations arise in relation to 'thank you' gifts for participants, and whether these are seen as recompense and reward, or, more dubiously, as incentives or payments that may have a coercive effect (Morrow 2009). As shown above, such gifts can be very helpful in drawing people into a study. Through repeated interviews participants may well come to anticipate such a reward, which brings a contractual element to the process. Nevertheless, given the longer-term commitment that QL research entails, and the time required for in-depth interviews, it is equally important to avoid economic exploitation. Some reward or recompense is fully justified in these circumstances, particularly for low-income participants. A gift voucher, for example, can be an important element in the reciprocal offer. Being transparent at the outset about the giving of such rewards and explaining their purpose clearly to participants helps to avoid the potential for coercion.

## Confidentiality, authenticity and shared authority

It is a cardinal principle of social research, embodied in ethics protocols and the UK Data Protection Act (1998), that researchers should not divulge identifiable information about participants to third parties (Moore 2012, Wiles 2013). The commitment to safeguard confidentiality is usually built into informed consent, thereby setting the standard for how a project will unfold. Re-assurances of confidentiality at this stage can perform a vital function in enabling participants to speak freely, without fear that their 'warts and all' accounts, views and experiences will be divulged to others outside the research domain. This in turn can enhance the meaning and authenticity of participants' accounts. Maintaining confidentiality, however, can be a challenge when the risk of disclosure is magnified over time. The cumulative generation of rich, biographical data creates a unique, holistic 'finger-print' for a participant, which is increasingly revealing of identities, localities and life circumstances (Hughes 2011). Even the simple process of re-contacting participants for a revisit needs to be handled with care (Laub and Sampson 2003, Miller 2015). Letters, Facebook messages or telephone messages may inadvertently reveal to third parties details of past or recent lives that participants may not have disclosed themselves, or may no longer wish to 'own' or be reminded of. In these circumstances, it may be best to allude to the research rather than discuss its nature (Harocopos and Dennis 2003).

Issues of confidentiality are also magnified in studies involving groups such as families, organizations and small-scale communities, for there is increased danger over time of information leaking across participants in the study, or finding its way into the public domain (Reiss 2005; Harden and colleagues 2010; MacLean and Harden 2012). Issues of *internal confidentiality* are endemic to all group-based studies (Macmillan and colleagues 2012; Taylor 2015). But for QL research they also arise where a group identity is forged across a panel of participants, for example, through shared web spaces or via focus groups or other events which bring the panel members together. These are common strategies to keep samples engaged (see above), but they require the panel to commit to internal confidentiality. A useful strategy is to issue ethical guidelines to discourage disclosures about fellow participants, which panel members can pledge to uphold (Patrick 2012).

The principle of confidentiality, however, needs to be balanced against the equally compelling drive towards authenticity and empowerment: that is, towards preserving the integrity of participants' accounts and enabling a more open identification of, and acknowledgement for their contributions. Regardless of the potential liberation that comes from speaking in confidence, participants may wish to give candid accounts in their own right, and to be acknowledged for doing so (Corden and Sainsbury 2007; Grinyer 2009). Increasingly, the imperative to anonymize data and obscure identities sits uneasily with the view that the process may strip a dataset of its integrity, diminish its intellectual meaning and scientific value and do a disservice to participants who are airbrushed out of the historical record (Moore 2012). One way of addressing the latter problem is to ensure that a full, unabridged dataset, complete with participant contact details, is carefully preserved in a 'dark' archive for eventual historical use (Neale and colleagues 2016).

While there are no easy answers to these ethical dilemmas, researchers need to tread a delicate path between confidentiality, authenticity and empowerment. One solution is to adopt the principle of shared authority and consult carefully with panel members over how they wish to be represented in research data and outputs. Imagining the participants as part of the audience for a published work, and reading it 'through their eyes' may help to ensure that research evidence is presented sensitively and with regard to participants' feelings (Ellis 1995). The need to consult about published findings or displays of data, particularly where they touch on sensitive issues, becomes all the more important where relationships between researcher and participants are built on trust and enduring commitments through time. In his longitudinal study of science teaching in a high school, Reiss (2005) gives a candid account of what might happen without such consultation. He underestimated how the identities of the teachers might unravel over the course of the study, and how easily his assigned identities could be decoded by other staff in the school. This was of great concern to the teachers, who were also upset at what they saw as an overly critical stance in the way that Reiss reported his findings. As he notes, a more respectful, consultative and collaborative approach at the close of fieldwork, prior to the publication of findings, could have averted these problems (see Chapter 6 for an example of a collaborative approach).[3]

## Reciprocity and professional boundaries

As shown above, maintaining a panel of participants over time is an important methodological issue for QL researchers. Ethically, however, the concern becomes one of sustaining and nurturing relationships (Pollard 2007). The process of walking alongside people, the sense of accompanying

---

[3] These experiences are not uncommon among longitudinal researchers (see, for example, Ellis 1995; Scheper-Hughes 2000 and Hermanowicz 2016). Ellis (1995) and Scheper-Hughes (2000) give striking accounts of the consequences of such problems in their longitudinal ethnographies of close knit rural communities. Scheper-Hughes' findings, which were published in the United States following a year of intensive fieldwork in an Irish community, were feted by academics but condemned by Irish commentators and local people. When she revisited the community after an absence of twenty-five years she was initially shunned by the villagers and then expelled. There was little sense of any shared authority in the way this research was conducted. As Scheper-Hughes acknowledges, it was marked by a lack of transparency about the aims and focus of the study, and the times when people were, or were not under scrutiny; a negative portrayal of the villagers and failure to write sensitively about the positive aspects of their community life; and a failure to consult over identities that were easily decoded by the villagers.

them on their life journeys, may touch the lives of both participants and researchers. Longitudinal ethnographers, for example, describe this process as a deep immersion, whereby they are, 'engaging ... with part of who they are' (O'Reilly 2012: 521; Burton, Purvin and Garratt-Peters 2009). Care is therefore needed in managing these shifting relationships over the course of a study and re-situating ethical practices where appropriate (Thomson 2007, Mauthner and Parry 2013; Taylor 2015: 283). The task involves building trust, mutual respect and reciprocity in ways that do not lead to over-dependence or involvement, intrusion or neglect, to the detriment of either researcher or participant (Pollard with Filer 1996; Birch and Miller 2002; Molloy and Woodfield with Bacon 2002, Reiss 2005; Morrow 2009). Sustaining relationships in these ways involves a balance between two ethical principles. The first is *reciprocity*, the notion of an ongoing 'gift' relationship, which is central to qualitative enquiry (Gordon and Lahelma 2003). The second is the need to maintain the *professional boundaries* of a research relationship over time, along with a clear focus on the professional nature of the researcher role (Hemmerman, 2010; Hammersley and Traianou 2012). Projects working with different field methods and with differently constituted samples are likely to balance these principles in varied ways; there is no prescriptive approach that works in all research contexts.

### Giving and receiving support

The question of how much and what kind of support may be legitimately and appropriately provided – and received – as part of an ongoing, reciprocal relationship needs to be worked out in relation to local circumstances, contexts and cultures, as well as the overall time frame for a study (Morrow 2013). In an anthropological study of a Mexican community running over half a century, Foster (2002) was aware that his whole academic reputation, including the royalties from his books, had been built on the sustained research contributions of the local people. While his research benefited the villagers in non-material ways, making them feel listened to, special and valued, he explains that sustained material benefits, given indirectly rather than through direct payments, had also become an essential part of the reciprocal offer:

> I contribute substantially to such things as public lighting and school funds and my name routinely is found on the list of contributors to any village function. ... Each year I leave with the village priest a

substantial sum of money to be distributed at his discretion among the village needy. Altogether my continuing contributions have far exceeded any monetary profit to me from publications. ... I believe no one is worse off for our presence, and I know that some are better off. A few, without our monetary intervention in medical crises, would almost certainly have died. (Foster 2002: 273)

The Mexican families with whom Foster stayed in the village were regularly made welcome as guests to Foster's home in the United States. However, local competition for scarce resources also engendered competition for his favours. Some jealousies were directed at these 'favoured' families, which may have affected their close knit village ties (Foster 2002: 273–4). Foster's account reveals how, over many years, the professional researcher role evolved gradually and naturally into one of enduring friendship. These are common experiences among longitudinal ethnographers (Kemper and Peterson Royce 2002).

Whatever the local context, the longer the time frame for a study, the greater the likelihood that participants will need or request some form of support, or seek to reciprocate themselves. In the *Following Young Fathers Study*, for example, the researchers were asked to provide a character reference for a participant who was facing a custodial sentence. This raised a number of dilemmas: what did the researchers know, but also not know about the young man beyond the confines of the research relationship? Could they breach confidentiality? And could they vouch for the young man's moral conduct in a legal context? Keeping within the bounds of the research relationship, the team provided a general reference for the young man that outlined the valuable contribution that he had made to the research (Neale and colleagues 2015). On another occasion, the team offered some educational advice to a young participant whose interviews revealed a persistent and unfulfilled aspiration to go to university. The methodological drawbacks of influencing the life path of the young man were outweighed by the ethics of 'giving something back'.

Similarly, in a study of welfare reform, Patrick (2012) gave some rudimentary welfare advice to her participants. This was seen as a central part of the reciprocal offer: it would have felt unethical to refrain from providing advice that would materially benefit the participants, although in the process she was influencing their welfare journeys. On another occasion, a participant presented Patrick with a small gift for her new baby. To decline the gift would have been disrespectful and may have damaged the relationship. At the same time Patrick made clear her limited capacity to provide further support or to maintain contact beyond the end of her project. She also clarified the limits of her ability to influence welfare policies as an outcome of the project – something that had initially motivated some of the participants to take part in the study.

As these examples show, the balancing act between reciprocity and professional boundary maintenance requires some finesse, and it may become a challenging process in particular field settings. In a community study of low-income, disadvantaged families, for example, Hemmerman (2010) reports that maintaining the sample required frequent informal visits to the community, which ran the risk of intrusion and over familiarity. Reciprocity in this scenario meant supporting the households with basic chores and food shopping prior to conducting an interview. A sustained engagement of this nature can be emotionally challenging, particularly when researching sensitive topics. Hemmerman was affected by the precarious lives of her participants and the traumatic events that they shared with her. Similar experiences were reported by Calman, Brunton and Molassiotis (2013) in their study of terminally ill cancer patients, many of whom died during the study. In such circumstances, walking alongside participants can be stressful. This suggests the need for ongoing support for researchers, for example through a buddy system (Williamson and colleagues 2014: 86). More broadly, these experiences raise questions about the nature and extent of researcher involvement in the daily lives of participants. Whatever strategies and solutions are adopted, steering a path through over-dependence, intrusion, neglect and emotional entanglement will be eased where the boundaries of reciprocity and professional research relationships are considered at the outset of a study.

## Privacy

The privacy principle is closely allied to the need for confidentiality. It requires researchers to consider whether they are intruding into the lives of participants, and to what extent participants are being asked to disclose sensitive information about their lives that they may not feel comfortable with. The usual protocols of qualitative research enable participants to say as much or as little as they choose. Even so, privacy can quickly unravel over successive waves of a QL study, where building relationships of trust may invite greater intimacy. Moreover, what comes under the spotlight is not just the 'life as told' in the moment, but the 'life as lived', and how and why it is unfolding in particular ways. This requires some congruence between how a life is narrated to the researcher, and how it is unfolding. It is an inherently deeper, more reflexive and open process, which requires a greater level of commitment, integrity and willingness to disclose on the part of the participant. While some participants may welcome this and find it enriching, others will avoid it or find themselves unable to engage in this way, particularly at difficult times in their lives, or when they are not (yet) ready to share sensitive issues with a researcher (McLeod 2003: 206). Time can be a good resource here, giving some flexibility about when to touch on sensitive issues, and allowing them to be opened up retrospectively, when the dust has settled and relations of trust have developed further (Macmillan and colleagues 2012). In the *Following Young Fathers Study*, for example, issues relating to illiteracy, anger management, domestic violence and illegal activities were disclosed over substantial periods of time rather than at the outset, and often when participants could reflect on them retrospectively, as experiences that they could put behind them (Neale and colleagues 2015; Burton, Purvin and Garrett-Peters 2009).

## The extent of participation

The extended time frames for QL research open up the potential for participants to play a role in a project that goes beyond their conventional 'informant' role. For example, panel members may be invited to generate data themselves, to read and verify interview transcripts or case materials; to offer reflections on their past accounts from the standpoint of the present day; to act as consultants in the representation or the interpretation of data about their lives; and to contribute to dissemination and impact activities. In some cases, selected participants may opt to become spokespeople for the project and its findings, as part of which their identification in the research process may become explicit, requiring their confidentiality to be waived or re-negotiated. Overall, playing a more active role in a project can have a transformative effect on the confidentiality and privacy afforded to participants. In these ways, QL research shares some affinities with participatory and action modes of research, which are founded on the principles of empowerment, shared authority and the co-production of knowledge (Wiles 2012).

These extended forms of consultation and participation would seem to be commendable. As shown earlier, too little consultation runs the risk of breaching the principles of informed consent and confidentiality, with potentially damaging consequences for researchers and participants. On the other hand, too much consultation may also be problematic. The extended forms of participation outlined above raise questions about how far they should be taken, for which groups of participants, and in what specific contexts; there may be costs involved and unintended consequences. For example, involving participants in the production of written, video or audio diaries can be rewarding and interesting. But the process may also be too revealing, crystallizing aspects of a life that participants may not wish to share or would rather disown (Pini and Walkerdine 2011). The idea that such participatory approaches are necessarily empowering may be too idealistic. Researchers who commission such activities remain the prime audience for their production, and, in the process, their scrutiny extends beyond the interview into the realms of a participant's daily life (Pini and Walkerdine 2011). Similarly, where participants are invited to revisit their earlier interview transcripts this may carry emotional risks, for it involves a level of introspection that people may find uncomfortable (Miller 2000: 104). In this context, too, participants may find themselves confronted with seemingly 'fixed' versions of their past lives that they may no longer wish to identify with. In the ongoing flow of a life, past events and circumstances are continually open to interpretation as people selectively remember, change plans, modify aspirations, acquire new identities and overwrite their life stories (cf. Miller 2000; Thomson 2012). Being confronted with an earlier version of oneself may mean re-living old hurts or traumas, or it may reveal unfavourable comparisons between how a participant envisaged their future and what has actually transpired.

In the *Inventing Adulthoods Study*, for example, participants were invited to reflect on transcripts and video data from earlier interviews and analytical case histories that the researchers had subsequently generated. While some engaged happily in this activity, others expressed disquiet at the way they were represented or regretted their disclosures, feeling they were made to look stupid or otherwise exposed (although this was far from the intention of the researchers, McLeod and Thomson 2009: 75–6). In similar vein, Warin (2010, 2011) recounts how one of the teenage participants in her study of children's changing identities decided to drop out after he was shown earlier video footage of himself as a pre-schooler. He emphasized his maturity at the follow-up interview, and explained that he felt the study was 'too babyish'. Given the small sample size (ten young people), this was a serious loss to the study. Presenting people with a transcript or visual reminder of their past, or otherwise reminding them of what they previously said needs careful handling, for it may intrude on the internal process of 'reworking' the past. While QL researchers need to build cumulative understandings by comparing past and present day accounts, this does not obviate the need to respect the privacy of people's past lives, and to accept whatever version of the past is currently being conveyed.

Overall, it is possible that relatively few participants may wish to engage in the additional activities outlined above. Such extended roles may create additional burdens for them, taking them reluctantly into a process of reflexive interpretation of their lives – a quasi-researcher role – that they may find uncomfortable (Birch and Miller 2002; McLeod and Thomson 2009). Great care is needed to discern where participants stand on these issues. It has to be acknowledged that seeking to make the research process more democratic by sharing the analytical authority that researchers hold may be 'an ethical sleight of hand, even somewhat delusional' (Back 2007).

Balanced against such sensibilities, however, are the very real benefits for some participants in becoming ambassadors for a study, particularly when fieldwork is completed and they are able to move beyond their role as 'informant'. In the *Following Young Fathers Study*, for example, selected young men took part in a national practitioner conference towards the end of the study, where they contributed to workshops and formed a question and answer panel at the close of the day. This was a powerful means of giving the young men an audience as well as a voice. Their contributions were greatly valued by delegates and a matter of pride for the young men themselves. Using their own voices was immensely powerful and, arguably, carried more weight than the researchers' attempts to speak for them (Neale and colleagues 2015; Tarrant and Neale 2017). Their capacity to engage with practitioners was a significant finding of the study, but here it was not simply documented but actively demonstrated to a practice audience. Similarly, as part of a collaborative writing project, one participant produced an autobiographical account of his journey into fatherhood (Johnson 2015). In a subsequent impact initiative (Tarrant and Neale 2017) selected panel members went on to develop mentoring, advocacy and training roles under the aegis of a newly formed Young Dads Collective for the North of England (see Chapter 6). Such engagement clearly has the potential to empower and enrich the lives of selected participants, and it was also seen by the researchers as another way to 'give something back' to them for their significant contributions. Overall, however, such forms of engagement are not likely to suit all participants and are best seen as optional extras.

### Ethical closure

The time and effort needed to sustain ethical relationships over time are clearly substantial. At the same time they create extra challenges for bringing the research to a satisfactory conclusion (Reiss 2005). Marking the closure of a project, or the current phase where there may be a follow-up, is vital where participants have had a long-term commitment to a study. They may have a professional investment in the outcomes, or developed relationships and a research identity that they have come to value. A clear exit strategy is needed that goes beyond a formal letter or certificate of participation (Morrow 2009). Possibilities include a sociable event or a public gathering, exhibition or other form of dissemination event that participants can attend or contribute to (Neale and colleagues 2015; see Chapter 6 for an example). Or it may involve creative forms of output, produced in collaboration with selected panel members, and distributed to all as a fitting memento of their contribution (e.g. an anthology of participants' reflections or a collaborative film, Neale and Flowerdew 2004, Land and Patrick 2014). Such events and outputs, however, take foresight, time, effort and funding; a proactive strategy can help to build these resources into a study at the design stage.

## Concluding reflections

This chapter has focused on a central practice within QL research: that of walking alongside a panel of participants to discern how their lives unfold. The discussion has explored how participants are recruited into a study and how their involvement is best maintained. Strategies for re-tracing people if they become 'lost' to a study have been detailed, along with the need to temper the zeal of private detection with respect for people's privacy. The discussion illustrates how QL researchers are not simply maintaining samples: they become fellow travellers engaged in the crucial task of building and sustaining relationships. More than any other research strategy, this is the key to maintaining a sample. How this process is managed is the cornerstone of ethical practice in a QL study. For QL research, ethical literacy is an inherent part of the temporal landscape, a moral compass that helps to set a project on its course and navigate it as it unfolds. It relies on a mixture of proactive and reactive ethical strategies, drawing on pre-existing ethical protocols and shared knowledge, and creatively re-working them to address unanticipated ethical dilemmas as they arise. The domain of applied ethics is about making difficult choices in situations where no unambiguous options exist (Bishop 2009). While the longer time frames for QL enquiry magnify these challenges, time also operates as a resource in the resolution of ethical issues, and it may uncover and offer new insights into the moral terrain of participants' lives.

# 5 Journeys with data: Field enquiry and analysis

In common with other phases of the research process, generating and analysing QL data involves a cyclical and cumulative journey through time. These are intertwined processes that are structured through the tempo of a study. Likewise, the idea of QL research as a craft applies just as much to the process of working with QL data as it does to questions of design and sampling. There are endless opportunities for creativity here (Saldana 2002), alongside the ever-present need for careful design and precision. A dataset that cumulates through successive waves of fieldwork needs to have some internal coherence, while the sheer volumes of data that are generated require careful management to facilitate their analysis and longer-term use (a theme developed in Bishop and Neale 2012; Corti and colleagues 2014; and Neale and colleagues 2016). In this chapter, varied strategies for generating and analysing QL data are introduced, and the interlocking nature of these processes is explored. We begin by setting out four broad approaches to field enquiry: ethnography, interviewing, participatory approaches and the use of existing data sources. This is followed by a more detailed exploration of QL interviewing, and participatory tools and techniques. In the second part of the chapter we consider the distinctive momentum and logic of Qualitative Longitudinal Analysis (QLA).

## Generating QL data

There are four broad approaches to field enquiry that can be drawn upon and combined in the process of generating QL data:

---

**Ethnography**

This is an inherently temporal process, a core method used by social anthropologists, increasingly used by social scientists more generally, and commonly employed in QL research (see, for example, Corsaro and Molinari 2000; Pollard with Filer 1995; Burton, Purvin and Garrett-Peters 2009; O'Reilly 2012). Ethnography involves 'being there', 'walking alongside' people as fellow travellers (see Chapter 4). Ethnographers insert themselves to varying degrees into the lives of those under study, participating, observing, listening, asking questions (through formal and informal interviews), and gathering multiple sources of data to discern how people live, the nature of their world views and the tempo of day to day lives (Zerubavel 1979). Combining participant observation and interviewing through time gives longitudinal ethnography a particular strength: it can yield insights into how lives are being *lived* as well as narrated, and how both lived and narrated lives change over time.

---

**Interviewing**

This is the most widely used method for generating data in the social sciences. Qualitative interviewing typically takes the form of carefully planned, pre-arranged, in-depth discussions with individuals or small groups, although the encounters may be arranged spontaneously in the field. Interviews range from individual to group-based encounters, and from face-to-face to indirect discussions (by telephone or via the web, where they may be conducted in 'real' time or a-synchronically, with a time lapse in the conversation). A topic guide covering relevant themes and questions is commonly used to guide the process, while the resulting narratives are typically documented via audio-recordings that are transcribed to aid recall and analysis. The longitudinal frame of a QL study gives ample scope to combine interviewing with ethnographic techniques, e.g. 'walking' or 'shadowing' interviews (Thomson 2012; Bates and Rhys-Taylor 2017). This yields complementary forms of data and gives access to lives as they are lived, as well as lives that are told and retold through time. Interviewing strategies are explored further below.

## Participatory approaches

These are commonly combined with in-depth interviews. Data may be solicited or commissioned by the researcher, and jointly constructed or generated in a way that is participant-led. The tools used in this process may be visual (graphic, pictorial, photographic, video), or take the form of written or aural narratives. In QL research such data may be produced during or in-between waves of fieldwork, and, alongside their participatory potential, they provide a valuable focus for drawing out interview discussions. Participatory tools are explored further below.[1]

## Documentary and archival sources

Among the varied sources of data that underpin QL studies, documentary and archival sources have been relatively neglected. This is despite their potential to shed valuable light on temporal processes. A detailed consideration of these data sources is beyond the scope of this volume, but some salient points are drawn out here. Documentary and archival sources of data form part of a larger corpus of materials that Plummer (2001) engagingly describes as 'documents of life':

> The world is crammed full of human personal documents. People keep diaries, send letters, make quilts, take photos, dash off memos, compose auto/biographies, construct websites, scrawl graffiti, publish their memoirs, write letters, compose CVs, leave suicide notes, film

---

[1] A comprehensive review of participatory tools is beyond the scope of this book. For a discussion of life history charts see Neale 2017a. For visual and video methodologies used in temporal research see Pini and Walkerdine 2011; Frith 2011; Henwood, Shirani and Finn 2011, Bytheway and Bornat 2012; Mannay 2015 and Mitchell, De Lange and Moletsane 2017.

video diaries, inscribe memorials on tombstones, shoot films, paint pictures, make tapes and try to record their personal dreams. All of these expressions of personal life are hurled out into the world by the millions, and can be of interest to anyone who cares to seek them out. (Plummer 2001: 17)

Among the many forms of documentary data that may be repurposed by researchers, social science and humanities datasets have significant value. Researchers may draw on individual datasets or work *across* datasets to build new insights across varied social, generational or historical contexts (see, for example, Irwin, Bornat and Winterton 2012; Lindsey, Metcalfe and Edwards 2015). The growth in the use of such legacy data over recent decades has been fuelled by the enthusiasm and commitment of researchers who wish to preserve their datasets for historical use. Further impetus has come from the development of data infrastructures and funding initiatives to support this process, and a fledgling corpus of literature that is documenting and refining methods for conducting qualitative secondary analysis (QSA) (e.g. Corti, Witzel and Bishop 2005; Crow and Edwards 2012; Irwin 2013). A decade ago, debates about the ethical and epistemological foundations for reusing qualitative datasets were in danger of becoming polarised (Moore 2007). However, the pre-occupations of researchers are beginning to move on. The concern with whether or not qualitative datasets *should* be used is giving way to a more productive concern with *how* they should be used, not least, how best to work with their inherent temporality (Neale 2017b).

Many qualitative datasets remain in the stewardship of the original researchers where they are at risk of being lost to posterity (although they may be fortuitously rediscovered, O'Connor and Goodwin 2012). However, the culture of archiving and preserving legacy data through institutional, specialist or national repositories is fast becoming established (Bishop and Kuula-Luumi 2017). These facilities are scattered across the UK (for example, the Kirklees Sound Archive in West Yorkshire, which houses oral history interviews on the wool textile industry (Bornat 2013)). The principal collections in the UK are held at the UK Data Archive (which includes the classic 'Qualidata' collection); the British Library Sound Archive, NIQA (the Northern Ireland Qualitative Archive, including the ARK resource); the recently developed Timescapes Archive (an institutional repository at the University of Leeds, which specialises in Qualitative Longitudinal datasets); and the Mass Observation Archive, a resource which, for many decades, has commissioned and curated contemporary accounts from a panel of volunteer recorders. International resources include the Irish Qualitative Data Archive, the Murray Research Center Archive (Harvard), and a range of data facilities at varying levels of development across mainland Europe (Neale and Bishop 2010–11).

## Generating data through time: Continuity and flexibility

Before turning to a more detailed discussion of interviewing techniques and participatory tools, it is worth setting out some basic strategies for generating QL data in the field. Building cumulative data through the longitudinal frame of a QL study requires a balance between continuity and flexibility. Continuity is needed to ensure that an emerging dataset has some integrity and internal coherence to aid synthesis and analysis (Pollard 2007). A common strategy is to devise a set of core questions that explore key processes, themes, changes and continuities across the sample (e.g. 'then and now' or 'where next' questions, Saldana 2003; Smith 2003). These can then be revisited at each research encounter. To paraphrase Saldana (2003), this creates a *through-line* in the data, a thread that provides a synchronic link *across* cases and themes at any one point in time, and a diachronic link *within* cases and themes through time (Barley 1995; Smith 2003). These 'continuity' questions and forms of data provide the anchors for building an integrated dataset and aiding the process of temporal analysis. A 'baseline' questionnaire or checklist forms a useful component of a through-line, capturing structured demographic and circumstantial information for each case, which can be updated as a study progresses.

At the same time, the longitudinal frame allows for flexibility in how data are generated, and what lines of enquiry to pursue. As shown in Chapter 3, sampling strategies may involve expanding or condensing a sample (sample boosting as new dimensions of the research emerge, or funnelling in on particularly significant cases over time). The same logic can be applied to data generation. Over time, the researcher may 'funnel in' or progressively focus on themes of particular pertinence to a study or to a particular case or, alternatively, boost the scope of enquiry as new themes emerge (Smith 2003; Pollard 2007). A changing thematic focus is a common feature of QL studies, particularly where they are conducted over extensive periods of time or through varied phases of funding. Colson and Scudder's research among the Gwembe Tonga in Zambia provides a good example. Through repeated visits to the field over five decades, a conventional focus on the internal workings of kinship and ritual gave way to a concern with the resettlement of the community after the building of the Kariba Dam; the absorption of the Tonga into a larger political economy, and what this meant for their collective identity and citizenship; and more recently, the lived experiences of the Tonga in facing the AIDS epidemic (Scudder and Colson 2002; Burawoy 2003; Howell and Talle 2012).

A changing focus is not only a product of long-term field enquiry, however, for biographical and historical changes can occur in the moment. To give one example, in 2008, researchers across the *Timescapes Study* (2007–12) responded to the economic downturn as it began to emerge in the UK. They returned to the field armed with a new suite of questions about the recession and its impact on family fortunes (Edwards and Irwin 2010). The facility to ask new questions and to introduce new themes, building on insights from earlier waves of data and responding to changes in the social landscape, is a valuable feature of QL enquiry (Saldana 2003; Smith 2003). Taken together, continuity and flexibility are important strategies in the generation of QL data. Finding the right balance between these strategies is part of the rigour of QL field research.

## Temporal interviewing

Just as time provides a framework for generating data, it also shapes the nature of the data themselves. Here time comes into its own as a rich topic of enquiry that enriches the focus of enquiry and analysis. Interviews can be used to explore one or more of the planes of time outlined in Chapter 2: the flows of past, present and future; the interlocking horizons of turning points, transitions and longer-term trajectories; the interplay between micro- and macro-historical processes; the spatial dimensions of time (and/or the temporal dimensions of space); the oscillations of daily living, the pace of change, and continuities or ruptures in life experience. For example, exploring where people were born and have lived, who or what has influenced the direction of their lives, and what relational and socio-economic opportunities and constraints they have faced, will yield insights that span the micro–macro plane (Plummer 2001: 39–40; Miller 2000: 74).

In-depth interviews are commonly described as conversational, responsive, dialogical, open ended and so on. But the overall aim is the same: to gain insights into participants' subjective experiences, feelings and world views, and to build up a picture of how they construct, narrate and make meaning of their unfolding lives. The idea of narration, that people will have a story to tell about their experiences through time that can be drawn out and shaped through the research process, is central to QL interviewing. Life stories, Plummer reminds us, have the power to

> capture the continuous, lived flow of historically situated, pheno-menal experiences, with all the ambiguity, variability, malleability and even uniqueness that such experience implies. Whether this be the experience of being a nomadic hunter and gatherer, or a North American prostitute ... a worker down a mine, ... being worried to death in a nursing home, ... a teacher, or facing disability ... whatever may be of interest to the analyst, a key perspective is the participant's account of this experience. It may not be adequate on its own. But if a study fails to get this 'intimate familiarity' with a life, then such research runs the risk of simply getting it wrong: of speculating, abstracting and theorizing at too great a remove. (Plummer 2001: 37)

While interviews are not conversations in the sense of an informal, reciprocal exchange of news and reflections between two or more people, they are nonetheless conversational (in its original Latin, meaning *wandering or turning about together*) (Ritchie and colleagues 2014). Through this process, researchers and participants jointly construct meaning and knowledge as the interaction unfolds, enabling participants to find a narrative voice that explores and engages with meanings, rather than simply stating facts (Guenette and Marshall 2009). The resulting accounts are actively *generated*; they are not simply 'out there' in a realist sense, to be 'harvested' 'mined' or 'collected' from participants as if they are passive stores of knowledge.

Hareven (1982: 373–5) eloquently makes this point in her account of oral history interviewing:

> The interviewer is like a medium, conjuring memories through his or her own presence, interests and questions … [offering] a glimpse not only into the sequence of events in people's lives but how, in their search for a pattern, the different pieces of their lives are re-assembled and dis-assembled as in a kaleidoscope, losing meaning, changing meaning, disappearing, and reappearing in different configurations at different points in time.

Hareven observes that this constructivist, narrative understanding of data generation is part of its value. Rather than detracting from the integrity and meaning of people's accounts, these methods yield explicit interpretations, understandings and reconstructions of people's life events and circumstances, generating valuable insights into what matters to them at different moments and why (Hareven 1982: 374; Hammersley and Atkinson 1995; Ritchie and colleagues 2014: 180).

Biographical interviews may be conducted in a variety of ways (Thompson 2000; Plummer 2001; Miller 2000; Wengraf 2000; Merrill and West 2009). In a relatively unstructured approach, participants are invited to narrate their life, or segments of it, in their own way and at their own pace (guided very loosely by the researcher, for example 'how would you describe your childhood/family life/time in …? How did you first come to be involved with …? What was it like for you when you were growing up /starting out/ going through …'?) (Plummer 2000: 140–2). The aim is to elicit a spontaneous and relatively unmediated narrative. The biographic-interpretive method, for example, begins in this minimalist fashion, with one key question posed to set the life story in train (Wengraf 2000).

However, not all participants will feel able to respond to such a minimalist prompt, and the lack of guidance and interaction may serve to close down communications and empathy (Clausen 1998; Chase 2005; Brannen 2013; Thompson 2000; Merrill and West 2009). In some cases, a prolonged, empathic interaction may be needed to draw out a narrative, or creative tools may be needed to enable its articulation (Clausen 1998, Guenette and Marshall 2009 and see below). In any case, spontaneous narratives may well present a gloss on how a life unfolds, or, at least, a highly edited, partial version (Clausen 1998: 192). For this reason, researchers usually follow these unstructured phases of an interview with semi-structured questions that dig deeper to draw out key themes or fill in missing elements that are pertinent to the research ('tell me more about …' questions). This is the strategy used in the biographic-interpretive method of data generation (Wengraf 2000; Brannen, Moss and Mooney 2004).

## Life journey interviewing

A more gentle 'easing in' to an interview can be achieved by adopting an interactive and guided approach from the outset. A checklist of topics and themes, devised to guide the interaction, may be shared with participants at the start of the discussion or beforehand (Merrill and West 2009). A 'cartographic' interviewing strategy begins with an exploratory, surface mapping of a particular landscape of enquiry (Ritchie and colleagues 2014: 190–1). More focused questions then follow to explore the terrain in greater detail, before digging down to excavate underlying themes, meanings and reflections (here, 'cartography' shades into 'archaeology'). In this way the interview moves from concrete life events and experiences to more reflective and abstract insights and interpretations. From the outset, this approach is grounded transparently in the themes of a study, which provide the focus for discussion. Yet this still gives participants space to construct their narratives in their own way. And it is likely to achieve the same depth of insight into what matters to them: how salient a particular process or experience is in shaping the course of their lives and its relative significance in relation to other influences and concerns.

In QL research, a cartographic strategy can be used dynamically to map and construct a life journey, building insights into particular transitions and trajectories, exploring how participants have arrived at the present day and how they envisage the future. Going beyond a simple mapping of a landscape, this approach explores the movement of people *through* a landscape, giving attention to both surface details and the depths and drivers of the journey. The starting point may be a general mapping of present-day circumstances located within the passage of time (identifying where people are on their temporal map, the nature of the current terrain, an outline of the paths they are following and how far along the paths they have travelled). This is followed by an exploration of the 'back story': how participants have arrived at the present moment, and the nature and meaning of the journey along the way. A number of dimensions may be explored in capturing past time: the pace, tempo, spatial dimensions or synchronicities of the journey; whether it was straightforward (linear), circuitous, meandering or filled with zigzags or peaks and troughs; to what extent it was planned, was anticipated or is living up to expectations; the opportunities and constraints (across the micro–macro plane) that have shaped the journey so far; and any mechanisms (trigger or turning points) that have provided the impetus for new directions or for reverting back to earlier paths. Finally, the interview may move on to explore how participants see their future paths, how they envisage 'getting there' (their plans, aspirations, hopes and fears, again shaped by external opportunities and constraints) and what this means for the longer-term trajectories of their lives. In this way the mapping of a participant's life is an inherently temporal process, which seeks to locate where people are on their subjectively defined life map, and explore the nature, meaning and interior logic of the journey as it unfolds.

In developing a life journey approach to interviewing it is worth bearing in mind that lives are rarely narrated in chronological order. For this reason, the construction of a biography is usually undertaken in the aftermath of the interview, as part of the analytical process. Moreover, the extent to which people envisage their lives as journeys to be planned and executed varies from person to person. As shown in Chapter 2, they may live in the moment, without a strong sense of agency over past choices or future directions. But a life journey approach can help to shed light on these different orientations to past, present and future, affording insights into the different ways in which people live in the steam of time.

### Recursive interviewing

The life journey techniques outlined above provide a strategy for drawing out the dynamics of lives in an in-depth interview. In QL research, the longitudinal frame for a study enables this process to be taken a stage further. As shown in Chapter 2, the unfolding lives of individuals or collectives are not fixed at any one moment, but are constructed, reconstructed and updated through the recursive spiral of time (McLeod 2003; Grbich 2009; Jost 2012). Through the tempo of a study, QL research can mirror and illuminate the processes through which people overwrite their biographies. Recursive interviewing involves looking both backwards and forwards in time, revisiting, re-visioning and updating a life journey at each successive interview. Participants are invited to review the past, update previous understandings, and re-imagine the future through the lens of the ever-shifting present (McLeod 2003: 204–5). This makes it possible to compare accounts of intentions and expectations with how events and circumstances actually unfold (Walker and Leisering 1998). This iterative approach to past, present and future offers a more nuanced and fluid way of exploring life course dynamics. In the process, time as the medium for conducting a study begins to merge with time as a rich theme of enquiry.

The value of recursive interviewing is that it takes into account and seeks to capture the flux of life – the recognition that the construction of a life is inherently provisional, and that people are perpetually in an emergent state of 'becoming' (Worth 2009). As Plummer (2001: 40) notes, contingencies, volatilities and inconsistencies are an inevitable feature of all unfolding biographies. Our lives 'are flooded with moments of indecision, turning points, confusions, contradictions, and ironies', which are likely to be reflected in the way lives are both narrated and lived. This is clearly recognized by participants themselves. It is reflected, for example, in the changing autobiographical account of Wladek (Thomas and Znaniecki (1958 [1918–21]: volume 3; and see Chapter 2 for further examples of re-visioning the past). In the *Following Young Fathers Study* one young participant reflected on his experience of creating and updating a life map and self-portrait over four waves of interviews:

> I bet you find I ... put loads of different answers. It just depends on how you are feeling at the time. ... To be honest, every time I've done one, I've come back to it and I've not even known what I've put, because your feelings and opinions change don't they? (*Jason, wave four interview, 19 Feb 2014, Following Young Fathers Dataset, Timescapes Archive*)

Researchers seeking a surface, 'factual' account of a life journey may be unable to detect the rich flux of life course processes, or may gloss over or flatten them out (Plummer 2001). Yet uncovering these intricacies and changes in perception is vital if the interior logic and momentum of a life is to be understood. Recursive interviewing, then, uncovers the constant state of flux in which lives unfold and, working with this dynamic, seeks to uncover how the narrative of a life, the life as told, is continually re-adjusted to the life as lived.

Strategies for weaving back and forth through time will depend on the focus of the study, the characteristics and circumstances of the participants, and at what point important themes, gaps or anomalies arise in a narrative that need greater attention. Researchers will need to decide how far back and forwards in time they wish to explore, and at which particular moments. It may be useful to start off with relatively small time horizons (the time since last interview, the last year, or a projection over the next year), before moving on to longer horizons that stretch into the more distant past or future. The time frame of a study itself can provide a temporal horizon. At the outset, participants can be invited to reflect on where they envisage they will be by the end of the study, and, at the exit interview, on how far they have come over the study period (Saldana 2003). A longer-term horizon offers more scope to explore personal, family and structural influences across the micro–macro plane, and is a valuable means of contextualizing the specific journey under study and discerning how it fits within the longer-term trajectories of a life.

In using recursive interview techniques, researchers need to consider how far and in what ways they will prompt participants about their past and future lives (drawing on knowledge gleaned in previous interviews), and to what extent this might influence or unsettle people's perceptions. For example, participants may be asked to simply recount where they were previously in relation to the present day, or whether their views of past or future have changed at all. It is not uncommon, at this point, for participants to seek clarification on where they were or what they were doing at last interview and to be given a gentle prompt ('you were waiting to hear about …', 'had just started/finished …', 'were hoping to go on to …'). But taking the recursive process a step further, researchers may also share with participants extracts from their earlier interview transcripts, or the analytical files relating to their case, as a way of exploring just how and why they may have moved on or shifted perspective (see, for example, the recursive workbook used by Thomson 2012). Taking recursion to this new level can be an effective means of capturing transformations in people's values, aspirations or identities, or their revised interpretations of the passage of time. However, responses to this exercise are likely to vary from enjoyment to indifference, and from hilarity to disquiet (Thomson 2012; and see Chapter 4 for the ethics of taking a crystallized version of a past life back to people). As Thomson (2012) observes, creating a feedback loop between participant narratives and research data and interpretations is a powerful intervention. It needs to be carefully considered and utilized only where it is mediated by trusting relationships and ethical sensitivity.

## Participatory tools and techniques

The process of QL interviewing is often combined with the use of participatory tools and techniques that generate complementary forms of temporal data. These include graphic, pictorial, photographic or video data and written or aural accounts (diaries/audio diaries or autobiographical accounts of past or future). With varying levels of guidance from the researcher, such data can be created in ways that are participant-led. A brief overview of key tools is provided here (a more extensive review can be found in Neale (2017a)).

### Life maps

These pictorial tools are also known as time maps or time lines, although they are not necessarily constructed in linear fashion. They capture an unfolding life in an easily accessible, visual format. Participants are invited to draw a simple map of their life journey (or a segment of their life) and to highlight key milestones, events, transitions and/or turning points along the way. They may choose to draw mind maps, horizontal or vertical lines, parallel lines representing different and overlapping pathways, or zig zag, criss-crossing, circular, spiral, or flowing paths that denote varied ups and downs, historical loops, cul-de-sacs or wandering journeys (cf. Zerubavel (2003: 1–36; and Iantaffi's rivers of experience 2011). Researchers sometimes suggest a straight line as the basic drawing tool (and, by implication, a linear and sequential vision of the life course). But even so, participants may deviate from this or add embellishments to map their lives in their own ways (for a range of examples, see Guenette and Marshall 2009, Worth 2011 and Van Houte 2017). The drawings may range over a whole life or varied segments of it, even down to a single day, and they can be used to explore the future as well as the past (Thomson and Holland 2002; Gordon and colleagues 2005; Worth 2011; Hanna and Lau Clayton 2012; Falola 2015). These tools serve a similar purpose to structured life history charts (reviewed in Neale 2017a), but life maps are personalised, intuitive and creative tools that reflect the fluidity of life journeys. They allow an understanding of emotional as well as event-based journeys, and, unlike life history charts, do not require accurate recall of the sequencing and chronology of events. Their simple construction means that they can be integrated with ease into a biographical interview, where they can enrich and deepen a verbal account (Worth 2011). They can also be revisited at subsequent interviews and used recursively to update or modify an existing life map. Overall, these are good tools to 'think with' (Neale 2012), simplifying complex ideas, opening up sensitive life experiences, encouraging self-reflection, and giving tangible, visual shape to an emerging biography in ways that would not be possible through a verbal exchange alone (Worth 2011).

## Diaries

Soliciting or commissioning diaries and related writings has a long history in qualitative temporal research and remains a popular research tool (Pember Reeves 2008 [1913]; Shaw 1966 [1930]; Plummer 2001; Bytheway 2011; Bartlett and Milligan 2015). In their very construction, diaries are temporal records, capturing the immediacy and intimacy of life as it is lived. Interior thoughts and feelings, alongside events and circumstances of significance to the diarist, are recorded in the stream of time, as they occur, providing a record of an ever-changing present (Plummer 2001: 48; Fincher 2013). In contrast to autobiographies (one-off, retrospective accounts that reconstruct and explain a life through a backward gaze, e.g. Johnson 2015), diaries work prospectively. They are constructed in the present moment and oriented to the future, documenting an unfolding life in an incremental and episodic way (Watson 2013: 107). Given their inherent temporality, diaries constitute a powerful form of longitudinal data. They derive their value from their intimacy, their seriality and their close proximity to the events they describe (Watson 2013). Since they are structured through time, they provide a lynchpin between past and future, following up on previous events, anticipating what is to follow, illuminating the intricacies of transitions and trajectories, changes and continuities. Capturing the processual nature of experience in this way can provide valuable continuity between waves of QL interviews, and give access to the minutiae of change that could not be gleaned in any other way (Bytheway 2012; Lewthwaite and Bartlett 2017).

In QL research, diaries are commissioned or solicited over a specified period of time, usually mirroring the process under study, and with the aim of capturing the ebbs and flows of daily lives, and/or key moments in a transition. Participants are given booklets to complete, with dates allocated to each page and clear guide-lines on themes of interest to the researcher. The entries may take a variety of forms, from the tick-box charts more commonly associated with structured time-use studies (Gershuny 2000), to free-flowing, hand written narratives (Bytheway 2012). In recent years, diaries have increasingly taken the form of multi-media (audio, video) or web based accounts (blogs or face book entries) (Monrouxe 2009; Pini and Walkerdine 2011; Fincher 2013; Robards and Lincoln 2017). There is a growth, too, in pictorial formats that can be used with young children or participants with limited writing skills (Wiseman, Conteh and Matovu 2005). Scrap-book diaries are creative inventions that encourage young people to blend written accounts with photographic records and memorabilia (Thomson and Holland 2005).

Diaries present some challenges, not least their variable quality and length, and entries that may be incomplete, un-dated, out of sequence, recorded in retrospect, edited or sanitised (Bytheway 2011, 2012; Watson 2013). Privacy is a key issue. Diarists may decide they have revealed too much and opt not to share their records (Thomson and Holland 2005; Pini and Walkerdine 2011). Perhaps the biggest drawback is participant fatigue: the process requires time, commitment and motivation that may not be sustainable beyond the short term. Despite the challenges, it is possible to elicit diary entries on a regular basis, particularly where participants have the time and inclination to write, where incentives are offered, and where researchers provide ongoing support, feedback and encouragement (Bytheway 2011, 2012; Monrouxe 2009; Bartlett and Milligan 2015).

## Future essay writing

Explorations of the future are integral to QL interviewing and commonly drawn out using life maps. But researchers may also solicit short written accounts of aspirations, plans, hopes and fears that can be drafted over a period of thirty minutes or so. In the main, these tools have been utilised in snap-shot, synchronic studies rather than in longitudinal enquiry (the *National Child Development Study* (1958 cohort) and the *Timescapes Study* are exceptions). In a pioneering study, Veness (1962) asked school leavers to imagine they were looking back at their lives from the vantage point of old age, and to write a life story that would span the intervening years. Similar tasks were set in a number of more recent studies, most notably in 1969 for the *National Child Development Study* (1958 cohort); in 1978 and 2010 for the *Isle of Sheppey Study and Re-study*; and in 2007 for the *Timescapes Study* (Elliott and Morrow 2007; Elliott 2010b; Pahl 1978; Crow and Lyon 2011; Lyon and Crow 2012; Winterton and Irwin 2011).

Writers may be invited to look back from an imaginary older life, as in the Veness (1962) study, or to project forward a number of years from the present day. The teenagers in the *NCDS 1958 cohort* and in the *Timescapes Study*, for example, were invited to imagine that they were twenty-five years old, and to write about the lives they envisaged leading at that age. For the *Timescapes Study*, the writings ranged from short note-form accounts produced during an interview, to more extensive scripts that were produced between interviews. Those produced independently were then mailed to the researcher, or brought to the next interview, where they formed the basis for further discussion. In this way, the researchers were able to locate the essays within the context of interview data about the young people's backgrounds and evolving lives (Winterton and Irwin (2011, also 2012)).

Written accounts of the future serve a dual purpose. They are reflections of the times in which they are produced, illuminating how aspirations are shaped by prevailing structural opportunities and constraints (Sanders and Munford 2008). They have been used to explore the construction of young people's identities, their projections for family, home, leisure and working lives, and the influence of structural determinants (class, gender, family background) on these processes (Hallden 1994, 1999; O'Connor 2006; Sanders and Munford 2008; Patterson, Forbes and Peace 2009; McDonald and colleagues 2011; Winterton and Irwin 2011). At the same time, these accounts have biographical as well as historical value. They can illuminate dynamic life course processes; how past and future are interwoven, and how aspirations and priorities for the future shift from the vantage point of different life course positions (O'Connor 2006; Crow and Lyon 2011; Sanders and Munford 2008; Patterson, Forbes and Peace 2009). Interesting insights have been reported on the mechanisms and turning points through which future paths are chosen, sustained or abandoned (O'Connor 2006; Crow and Lyon 2011). The extent to which young people plan out their future lives, or live with truncated time horizons in an extended present have also been explored (O'Connor 2006). Revisiting imagined futures recursively can shed valuable light on how far expectations of the future mesh with what actually happens. As shown in Chapter 2 imagined futures are not predictive of future paths. Yet their very construction can give shape to a range of possible selves and the pathways that may lead to their realisation (Worth 2009; Lyon and Crow 2012; Hardgrove Rootham and McDowell 2015). These accounts may, therefore, offer valuable insights into the seeds of change.

Like all writing tools, future accounts have their drawbacks. As is the case for written diaries, changing modes of communication in a digital age may constrain the use of what is increasingly seen as an outmoded form of communication (Lyon and Crow 2012). They have been used most effectively with young people of school age who are familiar with writing tasks (Veness 1962). The limited evidence suggests that they may be much less effective with adults (Henwood and Shirani 2012). The way this task is presented to writers requires care, for it can influence how far the accounts reflect thoughtful and relatively realistic expectations or shade into flights of fancy (for the latter, see Hallden 1994; 1999). The very wording of the instructions can make a difference (Winterton and Irwin 2011). Most researchers, from Veness (1962) onwards, have guided participants to write realistically about the future, using their personal experiences to imagine how they see their own lives unfolding. This generally works well, with researchers acknowledging the powerful and compelling insights that such writings can reveal (Pahl 1978; Crow and Lyon 2011).

## Constructing a tool kit

The approaches, tools and techniques used to generate QL data form a rich palette of complementary methods that can be combined in creative ways. There is scope to introduce new tools or refine techniques over time, while some researchers offer a menu of creative tools to engage the interest of participants (Saldana 2003; Weller 2011). Interview methods are commonly combined with life maps and/or written or audio diaries to enrich temporal insights and help sustain participant involvement and interest (Gordon and colleagues 2005; Monrouxe 2009; Worth 2011; Bytheway 2012; Neale and colleagues 2015). These varied data sources give access to different temporalities, interweaving past and future and working across varied horizons and tempos of time. As a prime example, Bornat and Bytheway (2010) combined life history interviews with diary techniques in their study of *The Oldest Generation*. This enabled them to capture both extensive and intensive horizons of time: the long sweep of lives lived over decades of change, alongside the contingencies of everyday existence for those in deep old age.

On a final note, it is worth bearing in mind that participatory life mapping and writing tools are rarely generated or analysed in isolation from a biographical interview (Zimmerman and Wieder 1977). Plummer (2001: chapter 3) aptly describes them as accessories to a life story, which can be contextualized within a larger dataset and used as a springboard for further discussion and reflection. Overall, if the rigour of QL enquiry is to be maintained, data generation techniques and tools need to be carefully chosen and piloted, taking into account the design and sampling decisions that shape a study. This should help to ensure that participants (and researchers) are not overloaded by a plethora of different activities that complicate field enquiry and present extra challenges for analysis, particularly when working with large samples or across varied settings. Similarly, where new field tools are introduced in subsequent waves, this can result in a loss of continuity and reduce the capacity for comparative data analysis over time. To avoid these pitfalls, most QL researchers work with a core interview/ethnographic approach, within which a discrete number of carefully selected participatory tools are utilized.

## Qualitative longitudinal analysis

Of all the dimensions of QL research practice, analysis is the most complex and the least well documented. Building interpretations that can shed new light on the social world has traditionally been seen as an obscure and 'esoteric process, shrouded in intellectual mystery', or as largely serendipitous or 'haphazard, with discovery falling from the evidence as if somehow by chance' (Ritchie and Lewis 2003: 199). While researchers need a clear logic and rationale for their approach, there are no cast iron rules or procedures for QLA. Strategies vary from project to project (see, for example, Saldana 2003; Lewis 2007; Thomson 2007; Hermanowicz 2016; and Vogl and colleagues 2017). They may also evolve within a project (Henderson and colleagues 2012), or multiple analytical strategies may be employed in tandem for different cohorts and sub-samples (Calman, Brunton and Molassiotis 2013). In the main, QLA draws on generic modes of case and thematic analysis, which are nested within an overarching temporal framework. As shown in Chapter 3, the conceptual logic of working across cases, themes and time provides the foundation for temporal sampling. Here this same logic is used to shape the analytical process. A variety of specialist analytical tools and techniques that lend themselves well to temporal enquiry may also be employed. Framework analysis (described below) is perhaps the most widely used. But narrative forms of analysis (broadly focused on the content and/or structural sequencing and progression of a life story), IPA (Interpretative Phenomenological Analysis) and grounded theorizing have also been adopted in a range of studies (Eisenhardt 1995; Plummer 2001; Ritchie and Lewis 2003; Andrews, Squire and Tamboukou 2008; Rapley 2016; Hermanowicz 2016). In our discussion below, the conceptual scaffolding that supports the analytical process is outlined. The distinctive momentum and logic of QLA is then introduced, along with a range of summative and descriptive tools that can help to structure the process.

## Conceptual scaffolding

Qualitative analysis in general can be conceived of as a conceptual journey that leads from summative to descriptive to explanatory accounts, and from finely grained to broader understandings of social processes (Saldana 2003). This is an iterative process that requires the researcher to move back and forth between different levels of abstraction, and to make a conceptual leap from description to interpretation. Qualitative analysis has been characterized as 'a loop-like pattern of multiple rounds of revisiting the data as additional questions emerge, new connections are unearthed, and more complex formulations develop, along with a deepening understanding of the material. ... [It is] fundamentally an iterative set of processes' (Berkowitz, cited in Srivastava and Hopwood (2009: 77)). This is a fitting description of the analytical journey in QLA.

A range of analytical tools that summarize, describe and reorder QL data can be used to support QLA. Taking the form of case files, diagrams, tables, charts, grids and so on, these tools perform a vital function. The size and complexity of a QL dataset makes it necessary to condense or summarize data into manageable proportions and synthesize them into new configurations, while, at the same time, ensuring that these condensed readings retain the integrity and meaning of the original data (Gale and colleagues 2013). This process enables the researcher to 'see' the dataset as a whole, and to read across the data in new ways. As part of the analytical journey, summarizing and describing dynamic processes represents the rather prosaic, mechanical end of temporal analysis (described by Molloy and Woodfield, with Bacon 2002, and in some detail by Saldana 2003). As Saldana (2003: 63–4; 158) acknowledges, however, this is just the first step in the process of reaching higher-level explanatory insights into the *how and why* of continuity and change. As many researchers observe, however, no tools of the trade can produce these higher-level insights. This relies on the interpretive skills of the researcher. QL researchers commonly report the value of regular analytical discussions (workshops, research away days etc.) that are designed to share and debate emerging insights and to sharpen thinking. The whole process requires 'a mix of creativity and systematic searching, a blend of inspiration and diligent detection' (Ritchie and Lewis 2003: 199).

It is useful to conceive of this analytical journey as a conceptual ladder or scaffolding (Mills 1959: 43; Wengraf 2000: 142–3; Ritchie and Lewis 2003: 212–17). Researchers move iteratively up and down the scaffolding, drawing on empirical data at the lower levels to create summary and descriptive files, which then form the basis for higher-level insights and understandings. At the higher levels, new insights can be tested against wider knowledge and evidence (external verification), before moving back down the scaffolding to check them against the original data (internal verification). The degree of 'fit' between the newly emerging evidence and pre-existing evidence is a central focus, made possible through the process of 'shuttling up and down the scaffolding' (Wengraf 2000: 142). In this way, emerging explanatory accounts engage with pre-existing theories and evidence, but remain empirically grounded.

## The distinctive momentum and logic of QLA

QLA has a distinctive momentum and logic, both of which are shaped by time. The *momentum* of QLA grows over the time frame of a study. Temporal analysis culminates in the formal, dedicated stage of analysis that follows the completion of fieldwork. But it is not confined to this stage. It is a cumulative and dynamic process that builds incrementally through the tempo of a study, structured through each wave of fieldwork. As the dataset grows, temporal patterns begin to emerge in the data: synchronic 'snap-shot' readings, where data appear 'frozen' in time (Barley 1995), are transformed into diachronic, 'processual' readings, that look both forwards and backwards in time (Neale and Flowerdew 2003: 194). This integration of synchronic and diachronic understandings is the foundation for temporal analysis (Barley 1995; Thomson and Holland 2003; Vogl and colleagues 2017).

The *logic of QLA* involves working across *cases, themes and time* to discern their complex intersections. The process is iterative and multidimensional, involving multiple readings of the data that requires the researcher to switch the analytical gaze. Each reading involves an interrogation of cases, themes and time, but from a different starting point that offers a distinctive window onto a dataset. These different readings (case/thematic/temporal) can be seen as three 'axes of comparison' (Barley 1995). Taken together, they enable the multiple facets of the dataset to be discerned, facilitating holistic insights into dynamic processes, and creating a balance between breadth and depth of vision, and between short and longer-term time horizons. These different ways of reading QL data are explored further below. It is worth noting that researchers usually work out a number of structured steps to analysis to suit their own studies (see, for example, Lewis 2007; Vogl and colleagues 2017). The process described below begins with case-led analysis, is followed by thematic analysis, and culminates in a full-scale integrative analysis of a dataset. In practice, however, these processes unfold in parallel, and gradually begin to merge as the analysis reaches fruition.

### Case analysis

This is an in-depth, within-case reading of data. Whether a case is an individual, family, organization or other collective, it can be seen as a discrete entity and analysed in its own right. The approach is comparative, drawing on and bringing together segments of case data gathered at different points in time to build a diachronic understanding. By re-ordering the data, discursive accounts can be turned into chronologically ordered case profiles (Eisenhardt 1995; Bertaux and Delcroix 2000; Miller 2000: 19; Thomson 2007). Researchers may analyse each case independently before comparing cases across a sample (the IPA strategy), or seek an overview of the dataset as whole before a more detailed reading of individual cases (the Framework approach). They may work intuitively, marking up selected texts and scribbling margin notes (IPA), or systematically, working line by line through each case (Framework). Tools to support case analysis (both summative and descriptive) are outlined below.

---

### Case analysis tools

**Summary mapping tools: Pen portraits.** These are short (one or two page) documents that capture a brief history of each case. Scripted by the researcher, the portraits are constructed chronologically, with clear headings for fieldwork waves. They serve to condense and highlight key topics, circumstances and developments in the life of an individual or collective. Since it is surprisingly easy to lose track of the cases in a sample, these condensing tools fulfil a vital role. They can also be used as appendices in reports and published writings to give an overview of the sample (e.g. Neale and colleagues 2015, Appendix 5).

**Descriptive tools: Case profiles/histories.** These descriptive tools create more extensive chronological reconstructions of individual or collective lives. Drawn from varied sources (interview transcripts, field notes, participatory data) and allowing for 'thick description' they present an in-depth, holistic picture of how a case unfolds (Geertz 1973; Smith 2003; Thomson and Holland 2003). They may incorporate the 'back' story and future hopes and plans, and provide a valuable means of charting how perceptions of past and future change through the study time frame. Like pen portraits, case profiles are commonly organised by wave, with thematic sub-headings. This creates 'through lines' in the narrative that can be pulled out for detailed investigation (Saldana 2003). As descriptive tools, case profiles are closely aligned with and retain the integrity of the original dataset. For example, key quotations from transcripts may be inserted, and page references to transcripts are commonly added to cross-reference the profile with the participant's own accounts. A suite of case profiles may be built up over time, providing the basis for comparison across the cases in the sample.

Descriptive case profiles may be elaborated into **case histories** that incorporate researchers' subjective reflections, speculations and emerging insights (Thomson 2007, 2010, 2011, Henderson and colleagues 2012; Brandon, Philip and Clifton 2017). These insights may be woven directly into a script, or appear in margin notes, appendices or coloured fonts. In this way, these tools feed into the development of higher-level interpretations, providing a valuable record of researchers' evolving interpretations over time (Thomson and Holland 2003).

Whatever the level of detail included in case files, they need to fulfil the task of condensing data to make it more manageable (Smith 2003; Thomson 2010b). Lengthy files that duplicate rather than complement the original data may have reduced analytical value, while the time and resources needed for their construction may prove prohibitive.

## Thematic analysis

This is a broader, cross-case reading of thematic data. Key themes, topics and substantive patterns of meaning are drawn out, and related data are brought together into thematic bundles. The themes may be descriptive, conceptual or temporal in nature (e.g. past, future, turning points). QL themes are likely to have dynamic, recurring or cumulative significance. For example, a concern with employment is likely to be framed in terms of employment pathways or trajectories. The labelling, sifting and re-grouping of data is guided by a list of core themes and sub-themes (thematic codes), derived from the research questions, conceptual road map and interview guide. The thematic list may be refined inductively through a systematic reading of selected interview transcripts. Tools to support thematic analysis are outlined below.

### Thematic analysis tools

**QDA software** tools such as NVivo and Dedoose aid the process of labelling, sifting and regrouping data into new thematic configurations. This requires a systematic, line by line reading and marking up of the data, using a list of thematic codes to guide the process. Working with a modest number of broad thematic codes will help to ensure that data are not fragmented and decontextualized through the coding process.

**Summary mapping tools: thematic charts.** These tools are 'ready reckoners' that give a graphic display of dynamic circumstances across the whole sample over the study time frame. They perform a vital condensing function, enabling researchers to quickly grasp the core themes of the study across the whole sample and over the study time frame. They can be used to identity dynamic patterns in the data that need more detailed investigation (Saldana 2003). In the *Following Young Fathers Study*, for example, a series of thematic charts were produced that enabled the researchers to see, at a glance, how many of the young men had sustained contact with their children over the course of the study, and the nature, stability or volatility of their education, employment and housing trajectories (Saldana 2003; Neale and colleagues 2015 Appendices 2 and 3). These charts can be constructed using Framework or other QDA software, Microsoft office software, or manually.

**Descriptive tools: Framework grids.** These structured tools are particularly suited to three dimensional temporal analyses (Ritchie and Lewis 2003; Lewis 2007; Corden and Nice 2007; Parkinson et al. 2016). Developed initially by NATCEN, they have since been incorporated into NVivo QDA software, but can also be constructed manually on sheets of A3 paper, or using Microsoft Word or Excel software (Swallow, Newton and Van Lottum 2003).[2]

The grids can be configured in varied ways to suit the focus and design of a study (see, for example, Molloy and Woodfield with Bacon 2002; Lewis 2007; Neale and colleagues 2015; Grossoehme and Lipstein 2016; Brandon, Philip and Clifton 2017). The general aim is to map key themes against cases and time periods (Lewis 2007). A separate grid is constructed for each key theme. A grid for housing journeys, for example, lists cases along the vertical axis, and time periods along the horizontal axis. Each cell is filled in with summaries of housing data, ideally with page references

---

[2] At the time of writing, researchers report that NVivo Framework software is not stable enough to facilitate shared analysis across a research team, necessitating the construction or reconstruction of the grids in other formats.

to transcripts. The data can be read in varied ways: a vertical reading discerns varied housing circumstances across the cases in the sample at each point in time; a horizontal reading discerns how housing journeys unfold for each case through time; while a combined 'diagonal' reading compares varied housing journeys across the whole sample through time (for an example see Neale and colleagues 2015, Appendix 6). This facility for multiple readings of the data can support the development of higher-level interpretations. It is also possible to construct grids for each case in a study (with themes mapped against time periods) (for examples, see Neale and colleagues 2015, Appendix 6; and Grossoehme and Lipstein 2016).

## Integrative analysis

This is a cross-cutting reading of case, thematic and temporal data. As shown above, temporal analysis has its own momentum. It is structured through the tempo of a study, building incrementally through each new wave of fieldwork and involving iteration between synchronic and diachronic readings of the data. As a study progresses, the production of new data inevitably re-configures and re-contextualizes the dataset as a whole, creating new assemblages of data and opening up new insights from a different temporal perspective. In contrast to orthodox grounded theorizing, which seeks theoretical saturation and analytic closure (the point at which nothing new happens, Charmaz 2006: 113), the momentum of QLA produces an open-ended, kaleidoscopic view of social processes (Foster and colleagues 1979; Stanley, cited in Thomson and Holland 2003).[3] Since lives are continually under construction, new patterns and meanings are continually emerging for each case in the study.

A full-scale synchronic analysis of data after each wave of fieldwork is not likely to be feasible, given the time and resources needed for such a task (Calman, Brunton and Molassiotis 2013). Nor will it be desirable. While some diachronic data on past lives and future aspirations will

---

[3] For a discussion of this theme in relation to sampling, see Chapter 3. However, not all grounded theorizing seeks definitive closure. See, for example, Charmaz (2006, chapter 6), whose theorizing is strongly interpretive and constructivist, and who has adopted the notion of theoretical sufficiency in preference to saturation.

have been gleaned at the baseline, its scope will be limited at this point. However, *an interim synchronic analysis*, based on a careful reading of interview transcripts, is needed after each wave to prepare the researcher for the next visit to the field (Smith 2003; Vogl and colleagues 2017). As fledgling themes, anomalies or puzzles in the data begin to emerge, they can be followed up at the next wave. Analytical tools can also be set up at the baseline wave, and summary or descriptive data added at each subsequent wave to flesh out the temporal picture. Over the time frame of a study, these interim synchronic readings gradually coalesce into a dynamic picture of social processes (Van de Ven and Huber 1995, Smith 2003, Lewis 2007).

The process culminates in a *full-scale integrative analysis* of the whole dataset as fieldwork is brought to a close. It is here that the conceptual leap is made from a largely descriptive to an interpretive level of analysis. Summary and descriptive data files are compared and synthesized holistically to discern similarities and differences within and across cases, across themes, through the time frame of the study and further back and forwards in time as appropriate. The analytical gaze oscillates between single and multiple cases, between micro- and macro-historical processes, between short- and longer-term time horizons, between transitions, trajectories and the fleeting mechanisms, drivers and inhibitors of change. Plausible accounts of dynamic processes may have already begun to coalesce from a dataset that is rich in descriptive detail and explanatory insights. But here the process is sharpened through a systematic examination of the whole dataset in relation to pre-existing evidence, and the construction of typologies or theoretical models of pathways and processes that fit the dataset as a whole (Ritchie and Lewis 2003: 244–8).

There are two further considerations to bear in mind when developing QLA. Firstly, the analytical tools outlined above offer varied and complementary ways of reading across a QL dataset. A combination of case, thematic and temporal readings is vital, and case profiling and matrix (framework) based tools are commonly combined (see, for example, Pollard 2007). But not all of the analytical tool kit and strategies outlined above will be needed for any given project. Researchers need to choose, adapt, combine and pilot these tools with care, ensuring that effort is not duplicated and resources not overloaded with the task of re-ordering data into many different configurations. In this way, a clear focus on the end goals of the analytical process can be maintained.

Secondly, whatever strategies are chosen to work across cases, themes and time and, thereafter, to shape the presentation of findings, these need to be tailored to the nature of the project. Researchers will need to take into account its epistemological groundings, the research questions that drive it and the design and sampling decisions that shape it, not least, the priority accorded to breadth or depth of investigation (see Chapter 3). For example, researchers working with very small samples, or using a psycho-social lens are more likely to structure their findings around individual cases, within which thematic and temporal insights are embedded (see, for example, Warin 2010; Thomson 2009, 2010a, Coltart and Henwood 2012; Compton-Lilly 2017). In contrast, those working across larger samples, in applied fields, or with a greater focus on micro–macro understandings, are more likely to structure their findings around particular themes, within which temporal processes and case-study evidence are embedded (Smith 2003; Lewis 2007; Henderson and colleagues 20007; Neale and Davies 2016). Both approaches have distinctive value and, despite their differences, are equally grounded in a commitment to explanatory depth.

## Concluding reflections

In this chapter we have explored the interwoven processes of generating and analysing QL data. Building a cumulative picture through the waves of fieldwork is essentially an iterative process, in which field enquiry is interspersed with periods of reflection and analysis (Peterson Royce 2005). As in other dimensions of the research process, this can be a challenge, requiring a mixture of continuity and flexibility, creativity and precision. A variety of field tools and techniques are available to support these processes, and to enable a rich accumulation of synchronic and diachronic insights. There is ample scope to combine elements from different field and analytical traditions, and to draw on new tools and techniques as a study progresses. At the same time, there is the ever-present danger that a field enquiry will unravel. Whatever tools and techniques are utilized, clear rationales are needed for their use, and they need to be piloted and chosen with care.

The analysis of QL data, with its multiple readings across cases, themes and time, creates particular challenges (Thomson and Holland 2003). It is a labour intensive and intellectually demanding process that requires a continual shift in the analytical gaze. But it is also exhilarating (Philip 2017). Building case and thematic data into an integrated whole, discerning how time is implicated in these processes, and gaining insights into the rich kaleidoscope of unfolding lives, takes the researcher into realms of lived experiences that are invariably unexpected and arresting. Whatever the challenges, it is an intensely rewarding process.

# 6 Looking back, looking forwards: The value of qualitative longitudinal research

This introductory volume has explored the contours of QL research, from theoretical underpinnings to research design and practice. In these concluding reflections the considerable strengths of this methodology are considered alongside its challenges. QL research has many compelling attractions, not least its capacity to discern change 'in the making' (Mills 1959). It can shed light on the human factors that shape lives, the varied ways in which transitions and trajectories unfold and how and why these pathways converge or diverge across a panel of participants. It can uncover the subjective causes and consequences of dynamic processes: the stability or inertia of continued states, the triggers and mechanisms of change, and the creativity, resilience and/or fragility of individuals and groups in shaping or accommodating to these processes. With its recursive power, QL enquiry captures how individuals overwrite their biographies, continually adjusting the narratives of their lives to their evolving experiences. In the process, the messy, complex, subtly shifting facets of human experience are brought to light (Farrall and colleagues 2014). QL researchers are able to:

- intensively 'walk alongside' people, in 'real' time, as their lives unfold;
- extensively follow them over decades;
- explore the journey along the way, as well as the destination reached;
- uncover the interior logic of lives and the dynamics of human agency and subjectivity;
- combine a palette of creative methods to capture the intricacies of life processes and the experiential dimensions of time;

- weave back and forth through time to gain a more processual understanding;
- investigate the triggers and mechanisms of change;
- discern the place of lived experiences within a broader landscape of social, historical or structural transformations;
- mirror real-world processes;
- flexibly trace, navigate and evaluate policy developments and interventions;
- create 'real-world' impacts as an integral part of a study.

This is cutting-edge research, offering creative ways to grasp the dynamics of social processes in a fast-moving world.

## Weighing the strengths and challenges

While the longitudinal frame of a QL study is a vital resource that offers many benefits and opportunities, it also brings challenges to the research process (Pollard 2007). Working with time is never straightforward, for it is a slippery and pervasive entity that can evade the precision of interrogation and defy neat, tidy, definitive categorization and explanation. The vantage point from which researchers and participants look backwards and forwards continually shifts: future time at the start of a study will have become past time by the conclusion (Krings and colleagues 2013). This requires a continual switching of the temporal gaze, placing intellectual demands on researchers. Added to this, the time frame and tempo of a QL study may not match the momentum of a participant's life, while the temporal window that a QL study affords may be a relatively modest one. Caveats may therefore be needed about the limited longitudinal reach of a study and how much it can actually reveal (Corden and Nice 2007).

The cyclical nature of the research process creates more tangible, logistical hurdles. Gaining consent, recruiting samples, generating, organizing and analysing data are not one-off tasks but recur repeatedly as the waves of fieldwork unfold. The process is intricate and the workload substantial and relentless. The cumulative nature of QL enquiry, with its forward momentum, complicates the process further. Maintaining a longitudinal panel, for example, is vital, yet this is likely to involve long-term ethical vigilance, and a commitment to sustaining relationships with panel members that may last for years. There are, too, the pressures of seeking ongoing funding to maintain a study and its core researchers (Pollard 2007). Certainly, the repeated visits to the field makes QL research an expensive option when compared to single-visit qualitative studies.[1] Moreover, the task of managing a complex QL dataset that accumulates through time can be overwhelming, as each new generation discovers (Foster and colleagues 1979; Saldana 2003). The contemporary issue of 'data deluge' has long been recognized among QL researchers. As Van de Ven and Huber (1995: xiii) observe, 'over time, data mount astronomically and over load the information processing capacity of even a trained mind'. Similarly, Pettigrew (1995: 111) warns of the danger of 'death by data asphyxiation: the slow and inexorable sinking into the swimming pool that started so cool, clear and inviting and now has become a clinging mass of maple syrup'. A rigorous approach to data management is all the more important in this context (Neale and colleagues 2016).

Finally, trying to maintain a robust study that is clearly-specified and well-structured, with identifiable goals and guiding questions, can be a struggle when key elements of the process may lose their clarity or be subject to revision along the way. In policy-related research, funders searching for solutions in rapidly-developing policy areas may drive the introduction of new themes and the abandonment of old ones (Corden and Nice 2007). This can create instability in the whole process. Overcoming these hurdles requires a balance between flexibility and continuity, and between creativity and precision in how a project is managed. The rigour of QL research is built upon this requirement. The time and resources necessary to meet the varied challenges outlined above need to be realistically appraised and built proactively into project planning and management. In short, QL researchers need an abundance of time, resourcefulness, sound organization, commitment, stamina, good luck and a dogged faith in the value of the journey and its eventual destination.

Whatever the hurdles, however, the benefits of working prospectively through time are beyond doubt. QL researchers are driven by an abiding concern for the changing fortunes of their participants, and a deep curiosity about how their lives are unfolding (Warin 2010; Compton-Lilly 2017). As shown above, the flexibility to follow lives qualitatively wherever they lead, to discern changing practices, perceptions and fortunes through

---

[1] To put this in perspective, the costs of QL research, even for medium-scale Qualitative Panel Studies, are modest in comparison to those of large-scale cohort studies (Pearson 2016).

the stream of time, and to address new issues and themes as they arise, gives QL research unique value. One of the main benefits of this method is the enhanced opportunity to produce iterative understandings of social processes. Iteration can be understood not simply as an instrumental, repetitive task, a mechanical form of feedback, but as a reflexive process of continuous meaning-making through which new themes, insights and understandings emerge (Srivastava and Hopwood 2009; Grbich 2007). Iteration can be harnessed in varied ways to spark and ignite new thinking, and to reach new meanings. It emerges, for example, through recursive understandings of past, present and future, and in the constant interplay between synchronic and diachronic readings, micro and macro frames of reference, and between existing theories and new empirical evidence. It is centrally embedded in the oscillation between researcher and participant understandings, and in constructive exchanges and collaborative working across the research/practitioner interface. All of these processes are opened up and enhanced through the longitudinal frame of a QL study. While these multiple, iterative readings cannot produce definitive evidence, taken together they can generate plausible accounts of dynamic processes as they emerge in particular contexts of time and space.

## And then what?

In his reflections about dynamic policy making, Ellwood (1998: 54) observes that 'when you think dynamically you must confront the "and then what?" question'. This broad question lends itself to many interpretations and responses, but it prompts us to consider a key issue: the destination of a QL study, in particular, the quality and credibility of its evidence, interpretations and findings, and its capacity to make a difference in the real world. These important areas of methodological debate and development have been touched upon in various places in this volume (e.g. above and in Chapters 2 and 5). But they have been given little focused attention by QL researchers and they demand further consideration (Calman, Brunton and Molassiotis 2013). To take one pressing example, QL researchers are well aware of the inherently provisional nature of QL findings and the lack of analytical closure that working through time entails. While these traits are common to all research evidence, they are made particularly transparent through the tempo of a QL study: 'each time you look, you see something rather different' (Stanley, cited in Thomson and Holland 2003: 237). The lack of analytical closure can create challenges in knowing when to bring a study to a close (Thomson and Holland 2003). Yet this is rarely construed as a problem (Farrall, Hunter and colleagues 2014: 75). The transformative nature of temporal data and insights as a study unfolds is part and parcel of its power. By its very nature it confounds the search for theoretical saturation and definitive conclusions. Instead it alerts us to an ever-changing kaleidoscope of lives 'in the making', perpetually unfolding through a complex and unpredictable web of events and influences. Nevertheless, the issue of analytical closure does suggest the need for new ways to think about the quality and credibility of temporal research evidence. Opening up debates about the 'temporal fixity' of QL evidence in what is, essentially, an open-ended form of enquiry, could have profound implications for how reliability and validity are understood in QL research, and what criteria are needed to judge the quality of temporal studies more generally.

It is worth flagging up a second dimension of the 'and then what?' question that is ripe for development. It relates to the potential for QL research to make a difference in the real world, and how this might be achieved. In policy-related research, QL methodology is increasingly used to evaluate health, social care and welfare interventions. Since the approach is flexible and grounded in real time developments, the longitudinal frame gives space to develop productive collaborations with policy and/or practice partners, and with participants themselves (see Chapter 4). Practice partners may play an active role in agenda setting, mediating field enquiry, steering future directions and disseminating findings (see, for example, Neale and Morton 2012; Neale and colleagues 2015). But these processes can also be taken further. In the 1970s, the research/practice interface was conceived in terms of *knowledge transfer*, seen as a linear, one way process. This subsequently gave way to the more interactive idea of *knowledge exchange*, and, more recently, to the notion of *knowledge co-construction*, an integrated approach which fosters practitioner-informed research, and research-based practice (Neale and Morton 2012). The appeal of this approach is that it encourages a sense of investment in and local ownership of a project, and provides the optimum conditions for the take up of research findings. With its extended longitudinal frame, QL research is ideally suited to facilitate the co-construction of knowledge with policy and practice partners. Working on the principle of shared authority also helps to avoid the ethical quagmires that, in some cases, have bedevilled the work of longitudinal ethnographers (see Chapter 4).

The *Following Young Fathers Study* provides an example of this approach. The focus of the study and the guiding research questions were developed in collaboration with local practitioners, who became committed partners over the six years of the project. Setting up a practitioner strategy group across a range of statutory and voluntary organizations also proved very effective, creating a forum for sharing ideas about policy and practice developments and for collaborative working. Embedding this study in a policy and practice landscape paved the way for a practitioner-led, one-year impact initiative, *Supporting Young Dads*, which followed on seamlessly from the empirical research. Co-ordinated by the research team, this initiative enabled the findings of the study to feed directly into new practice developments. Selected practitioners were able to pilot and test out new ways of working, particularly in developing sustained support for young offender fathers upon their release from custody. Practice partners also supported and trained selected young fathers as 'experts by experience' under the aegis of a new northern arm of the *Young Dads Collective*. The young men developed advocacy, mentoring and training roles, and tested their skills in training a variety of health and social care practitioners in how to engage effectively with young fathers (Tarrant and Neale 2017). This training is now being rolled out to other regions of the country.

Over the years, this grass roots developmental work has percolated 'upwards' from local and regional networks of professionals to national policy levels, helped by the engagement of the study team with the All Party Parliamentary Group on Fatherhood. The sustainability of such impact work is an issue, given current funding climates. Nevertheless, this initiative made a tangible difference to a group of young fathers and a range of leading practitioners and, of central importance, it helped to foster a wider culture shift in professional understandings of and responses to young fathers (Tarrant and Neale 2017). Overall, this study demonstrates the potential for QL enquiry to be used as a navigational device, running alongside new initiatives in real time, and working collaboratively to bring people together at key moments to take stock, review developments, and plan new ways forward. In this way, it is possible to create real-world impacts as an integral part of the research process, and to circumvent the oft-cited critique that, in a fast-moving policy world, longitudinal enquiry simply takes too long to be of value.

As a final consideration, Ellwood's question prompts us to reflect on future developments in this field. As an exploratory, flexible and creative methodology, QL enquiry is continually under development, offering exciting possibilities for generating new research agendas and refining empirical enquiry. Of particular note for the future are the possibilities for advancing mixed longitudinal methodologies; the growth in arts-based methodologies; the transformative potential of digital technologies for research design and practice, and their value as emerging sites of temporal enquiry; and advances in data infrastructures and methodologies for the preservation, discovery and reuse of QL data. The longitudinal frame, in itself, offers abundant scope for methodological innovation, for example, in building collaborative research relationships and networks over time, developing and refining imaginative research tools and techniques, and bringing creative and participatory forms of outputs to fruition (e.g. exhibitions, creative writing projects, and drama and film productions, see for example, Johnson 2015; and Land and Patrick 2014).

There is huge potential, also, for theoretical advances. The study of time in all its rich variety remains an open field, with scope for new explorations at the interface of temporal theory and research practice. These new agendas for QL research are likely to grow apace as this methodology assumes a more integrated role within the canon of longitudinal and life course studies, and as its place within the established fields of qualitative temporal research becomes more widely recognized. Researching qualitatively through time undoubtedly brings challenges. But, in the view of this enthusiastic advocate, these are far outweighed by the benefits. Engaging with time requires a leap into the unknown, a capacity to see beyond the visible. QL researchers may not know exactly where their research will lead, how long it may last, or what they may find, but they are likely to uncover some compelling insights along the way. In a variety of creative ways QL research does more than investigate dynamic processes; it responds to changes in the environments under study (Vogl and colleagues 2017). Perhaps above all else, it is this capacity to walk alongside a panel of participants and respond with sensibility to the rich flux of human experience that makes for a uniquely powerful and rewarding research journey.

# References

Abbott, A. (2001) *Time matters: On theory and method*, Chicago, University of Chicago Press.

Abrams, P. (1982) *Historical sociology*, Ithaca, Cornell.

Adam, B. (1990) *Time and social theory*, Cambridge, Polity.

Adam, B. and Groves, C. (2007) *Future matters: Action, knowledge, ethics*, Boston, Brill.

Agar, M. (1980) *The professional stranger*, London, Academic Press.

Alheit, P. (1994) 'Everyday time and life time: On the problems of healing contradictory experiences of time', *Time and Society*, 3, 3, 305–19.

Andrews, M. (2007) *Shaping history: Narratives of political change*, Cambridge, Cambridge University Press.

Andrews, M. (2008) 'Never the last word: Revisiting data', in M. Andrews, C. Squire and M. Tamboukou (eds) *Doing narrative research*, London, Sage, 86–101.

Andrews, M., Squire, C. and Tamboukou, M. (2008) (eds) *Doing narrative research*, London, Sage.

Back, L. (2007) *The art of listening*, Oxford, Berg.

Baraitser, L. (2013) 'Mush time: Communality and the temporal rhythms of family life', *Families, Relationships and Societies*, 2, 1, 147–53.

Barley, S. (1995) 'Images of imaging: Notes on doing longitudinal fieldwork', in G. Huber and A. Van de Ven (eds) *Longitudinal field research methods*, London, Sage, 1–37.

Barnard, A. (2012) 'Widening the net: Returns to the field and regional understandings', in S. Howell and A. Talle (eds) *Returns to the field: Multi-temporal research and contemporary anthropology*, Bloomington, Indiana University Press, 230–49.

Bartlett, R. and Milligan, C. (2015) *What is diary method?* London, Bloomsbury.

Bastian, M. (2014) 'Time and community: A scoping study' *Time and Society*, published online 2.4.2014.

Bates, C. and Rhys-Taylor, A. (2017) (eds) *Walking through social research*, London, Routledge.

Bell, C. and Newby, H. (1971) *Community studies*, London, George Allen and Unwin.

Bertaux, D. (ed.) (1981) *Biography and society: The life history approach in the social sciences*, London, Sage.

Bertaux, D. and Delcroix, C. (2000) 'Case histories of families and social processes', in P. Chamberlayne, J. Bornat and T. Wengraf (eds) *The turn to biographical methods in social science*, London, Routledge, 71–89.

Berthoud, R. (2000) 'Introduction: The dynamics of social change', in R. Berthoud and J. Gershuny (eds) *Seven years in the lives of British families*, Bristol, Policy Press, 1–20.

Berthoud, R. and Gershuny, J. (2000) (eds) *Seven years in the lives of British families: Evidence on the dynamics of social change from the 'British Household Panel Survey'*, Bristol, Policy Press.

Birch, M. and Miller, T. (2002) 'Encouraging participation: Ethics and responsibilities', In M. Mauthner, M. Birch, J. Jessop and T. Miller (eds) *Ethics in qualitative research*, London, Sage, 91–106.

Bishop, L. (2009) 'Ethical sharing and re-use of qualitative data', *Australian Journal of Social Issues*, 44, 3, 255–72.

Bishop, L. and Kuula-Luumi, A. (2017) 'Revisiting qualitative data reuse: A decade on', *SAGE Open*, January–March, 1–15.

Bishop, L. and Neale, B. (2010) 'Sharing qualitative and qualitative longitudinal data in the UK: Archiving strategies and development' *IASSIST Quarterly* (IQ), 34, 3–4 and 35, 1–2, 23–9.

Bishop, L. and Neale, B. (2012) *Data management for qualitative longitudinal researchers*, Timescapes Methods Guide Series, no. 17, www.timescapes.leeds.ac.uk.

Blows, E., Bird, L., Seymour, J. and Cox, K. (2012) 'Liminality as a framework for understanding the experience of cancer survivorships: A literature review', *Journal of Advanced Nursing*, 68, 10, 2155–64.

Bootsmiller, B., Ribisi, K., Mowbray, C., Davidson, W., Walton, M. and Herman, S. (1998) 'Methods of ensuring high follow up rates: Lessons from a longitudinal study of dual diagnosis participants', *Substance Use and Misuse*, 33, 13, 2665–85.

Bornat, J. (2004) 'Oral history', in C. Seale, G. Giampietro, J. Gubrium and D. Silverman (eds) *Qualitative research practice*, Concise paperback edn., London, Sage, 34–47.

Bornat, J. (2008) 'Biographical methods', in P. Alasuutari, L. Bickman and J. Brannen (eds) *The Sage handbook of social research methods*, London, Sage, 344–56.

Bornat, J. (2013) 'Secondary analysis in reflection: Some experiences of re-use from an oral history perspective', *Families, Relationships and Societies*, 2, 2, 309–17, Open Space on QSA.

Bornat, J. and Bytheway, W. (2008) 'Tracking the lives of the oldest generation', *Generation Review*, 18, 4.

Bornat, J. and Bytheway, W. (2010) 'Perceptions and presentations of living with everyday risk in later life', *British Journal of Social Work*, 40, 4, 1118–34.

Brandon, M., Philip, G. and Clifton, J. (2017) *Counting fathers in: Understanding men's experiences of the child protection system*, University of East Anglia, Centre for Research on Children and Families.

Brannen, J. (2006) 'Cultures of intergenerational transmission in four generation families', *Sociological Review*, 54, 1, 133–55.

Brannen, J. (2013) 'Life story talk: Some reflections on narrative in qualitative interviews', *Sociological Research Online*, 18, 2, 15.

Brannen, J., Moss, P., and Mooney, A. (2004) *Working and caring over the twentieth century*, London, Palgrave.

Brannen, J. and Nilsen, A. (2002) 'Young people's time perspectives: From youth to adulthood', *Sociology*, 36, 3, 513–37.

Broad, R. and Fleming, S. (1981) *Nella Last's war: The Second World-War diaries of housewife 49*, Bristol, Falling Wall Press.

Bronfenbrenner, U. (1993) 'Ecological models of human development', *International Encyclopaedia of Education*, volume 3, 2nd edn.

Brunswick, A. (2002) 'Phenomenological perspectives on natural history research: The longitudinal Harlem adolescent cohort study', in E. Phelps, F. Furstenberg and A. Colby (eds) *Looking at lives: American longitudinal studies of the twentieth century*, New York, Russell Sage Foundation, 219–44.

Bryant, R. (2016) 'On critical times: Return, repetition and the uncanny present', *History and Anthropology*, 27, 1, 19–31.

Burawoy, M. (2003) 'Revisits: An outline of a theory of reflexive ethnography', *American Sociological Review*, 68, October, 645–79.

Burton, L., Purvin, D. and Garrett-Peters, R. (2009) 'Longitudinal ethnography: Uncovering domestic abuse in low income women's lives', in G. Elder and J. Giele (eds) *The Craft of Life Course Research*, New York, Guilford Press, 70–92.

Bury, M. (1982) 'Chronic illness as biographical disruption', *Sociology of Health and Illness*, 4, 2,167–82.

Bynner, J. (2007) 'Re-thinking the youth phase of the life course: The case for emerging adulthood', *Journal of Youth Studies*, 8, 4, 367–84.

Bytheway, W. (2011) *Unmasking age*, Bristol, Policy Press.

Bytheway, W. (2012) *The use of diaries in qualitative longitudinal research*, Timescapes Methods Guides Series, no. 7, www.timescapes. leeds.ac.uk.

Bytheway, W. and Bornat, J. (2012) 'The oldest generation as displayed in family photographs', in V. Ylanne (ed.) *Representing ageing: Images and identities*, London, Palgrave Macmillan, 169–88.

Calman, L., Brunton, L. and Molassiotis, A. (2013) 'Developing longitudinal qualitative designs: Lessons learned and recommendations for health services research,' *BMC Medical Research Methodology*, 13, 14, 1–10.

Carlsson, C. (2012) 'Using turning points to understand processes of change in offending', *British Journal of Criminology*, 52, 1–16.

Chamberlayne, P., Bornat, J. and Wengraf, T. (2000) (eds) *The turn to biographical methods in social science*, London, Routledge.

Chaplin, D. (2002) 'Time for life: Time for being and becoming', in G. Crow and S. Heath (eds) *Social conceptions of time: Structure and process in work and everyday life*, Hampshire, Palgrave Macmillan, 215–29.

Charles, N. and Crow, G. (2012) 'Introduction: Community studies and social change', *Sociological Review*, 60, 399–404.

Charles, N., Davies, C. and Harris, C. (2008) *Families in transition*, Bristol, Policy Press.

Charmaz, K. (2006) *Constructing grounded theory*, London, Sage.

Chase, S. (2005) 'Narrative enquiry: Multiple lenses, approaches, voices', in N. Denzin and Y. Lincoln (eds) *Sage handbook of qualitative research*, 3rd edn., London, Sage, 651–78.

Clausen, J. (1995) 'Gender, contexts and turning points in adult lives', in P. Moen, G. Elder and K. Luscher (eds) *Examining lives in context: Perspectives on the ecology of human development*, Washington DC, APA Press, 365–89.

Clausen, J. (1998) 'Life reviews and life stories', in J. Giele and G. Elder (eds) *Methods of life course research: Qualitative and quantitative approaches*, London, Sage, 189–212.

Cohler, B. and Hostetler, A. (2004) 'Linking life course and life story: Social change and the narrative study of lives over time', in J. Mortimer and M. Shanahan (eds) *Handbook of the life course*, New York, Springer, 555–76.

Coltart, C. and Henwood, K. (2012) 'On paternal subjectivity: A qualitative longitudinal and psychosocial case analysis of men's classed positions and transitions to first-time fatherhood', *Qualitative Research*, 12, 1, 35–52.

Compton-Lilly, C. (2017) *Reading student's lives: Literacy learning across time*, New York, Routledge.

Conover, S., Berkman, A., Gheith, A., Jahiel, R., Stanley, D., Geller, P., et al. (1997) 'Methods for successful follow-up of elusive urban populations: An ethnographic approach with homeless men', *Bulletin of the New York Academy of Medicine*, 74, 1, 90–108.

Corden, A. and Nice, K. (2007) 'Qualitative longitudinal analysis for policy: Incapacity benefits recipients taking part in "Pathways to Work"', *Social Policy and Society*, 6, 4, 557–70.

Corden, A. and Sainsbury, R. (2007) 'Exploring "quality": Research participants' perspectives on verbatim quotations', *International Journal of Social Research Methodology*, 9, 97–110.

Corsaro, W. and Molinari, L. (2000) 'Entering and observing in children's worlds: A reflection on a longitudinal ethnography of early education in Italy', in P. Christensen and A. James (eds) *Research with children: Perspectives and practices*, London, Falmer.

Corti, L., Venden Eynden, V., Bishop, L. and Woollard, M. (2014) *Managing and sharing research data: A guide to good practice*, London, Sage.

Corti, L., Witzel, A. and Bishop, L. (2005) (eds) 'Secondary analysis of qualitative data', *Forum: Qualitative Social Research*, 6, 1 [Special issue on QSA].

Crow, G. (2002) 'Community studies: Fifty years of theorization', *Sociological Research Online*, 7, 3. http://www.socresonline.org.uk/socresonline/7/3

Crow, G. (2012) 'Community re-studies: Lessons and prospects' *The Sociological Review*, 60, 405–20.

Crow, G. and Edwards, R. (2012) (eds) 'Editorial introduction: Perspectives on working with archived textual and visual material in social research', *International Journal of Social Research Methodology*, 15, 4, 259–62.

Crow, G. and Heath, S. (eds) (2002) *Social conceptions of time: Structure and process in work and everyday life*, Hampshire, Palgrave Macmillan.

Crow, G. and Lyon, D. (2011) 'Turning points in work and family lives in the imagined futures of young people on the Isle of Sheppey in 1978', in M. Winterton, G. Crow and B. Morgan-Brett (eds) *Young lives and imagined futures: Insights from archived data*, Timescapes Working Paper no. 6, www.timescapes.leeds.ac.uk.

Dearden, G., Goode, J., Whitfield, G. and Cox, L. (2010) *Credit and debt in low-income families*, New York, Joseph Rowntree Foundation.

Dempster-McClain, D. and Moen, P. (1998) 'Finding respondents in a follow-up study', in J. Giele and G. Elder (eds) *Methods of life course research: Qualitative and quantitative approaches*, London, Sage, 128–51.

Denzin, N. (1989) *Interpretive biography*, London, Sage.

Desmond, D., Maddux, J., Johnson, T. and Confer, B. (1995) 'Obtaining follow-up interviews for treatment evaluation', *Journal of Substance Abuse Treatment*, 12, 2, 95–102.

Duncan, S. (2012) 'Using elderly data theoretically: Personal life in 1949/50 and individualisation theory', *International Journal of Social Research Methodology*, 15, 4, 311–9.

Du Plessis, C. (2017) 'The method of psychobiography: Presenting a step-wise approach', *Qualitative Research in Psychology*, 14, 2, 216–37.

Edwards, R. and Irwin, S. (2010) (eds) 'Lived experience through economic downturn in Britain: Perspectives across time and across the life course', *21st Century Society: Journal of the Academy of Social Sciences*, 5, 2, 119–24. [Timescapes special issue]

Edwards, R. and Mauthner, M. (2002) 'Ethics and feminist research: Theory and practice', in M. Mauthner, M. Birch, J. Jessop and T. Miller, (eds) *Ethics in qualitative research*, London, Sage, 14–31.

Eisenhardt, K. (1995) 'Building theories from case study research', in G. Huber and A. Van de Ven (eds) *Longitudinal field research methods*, London, Sage, 65–90.

Elder, G. (1974) *Children of the Great Depression: Social change in life experience*, Chicago, University of Chicago Press.

Elder, G. (1985) 'Perspectives on the life course', in G. Elder (ed.) *Life course dynamics: Trajectories and transitions, 1968-1980*, Ithaca, NY, Cornell University Press, 23–49.

Elder, G. (1994) 'Time, human agency and social change: Reflections on the life course,' *Social Psychology Quarterly*, 57, 1, 4–15.

Elder, G. and Giele, J. (2009) (eds) *The craft of life course research*, New York, Guilford Press.

Elder, G. and Pellerin, L. (1998) 'Linking history and human lives', in J. Giele and G. Elder (eds) *Methods of life course research: Qualitative and quantitative approaches*, London, Sage, 264–94.

Elliott, J. (2005) *Using narrative in social research: Qualitative and quantitative approaches*, London, Sage.

Elliott, J. (2010a) 'The "Social Participation and Identity Project"', *Ko'hort* CLS Cohort Studies Newsletter, Summer 2010, 3–4. www.cls.ioe.ac.uk.

Elliott, J. (2010b) 'Imagining gendered futures: Children's essays from the "National Child Development Study" in 1969', *Sociology*, 44, 6, 1073–90.

Elliott, J., Holland, J. and Thomson, R. (2008) 'Longitudinal and panel studies', in P. Alasuutari, L. Bickman and J. Brannen (eds) *The Sage Handbook of Social Research Methods*, London, Sage, 228–48.

Elliott, J., Miles, A., Parsons, S. and Savage, M. (2010) *The design and content of the 'Social Participation' study: A qualitative sub-study conducted as part of the age 50 (2008) sweep of the National Child Development Study*, Centre for Longitudinal Studies, CLS Working Paper 2010/3 www.cls.ioe.ac.uk.

Elliott, J. and Morrow, V. (2007) *Imagining the future: Preliminary analysis of NCDS essays written by children at age 11*, Centre for Longitudinal Studies, CLS working paper 2007/1.

Ellis, C. (1995) 'Emotional and ethical quagmires in returning to the field', *Journal of Contemporary Ethnography*, 24, 1, 68–98.

Ellwood, D. (1998) 'Dynamic policy making: An insider's account of reforming US welfare', in L. Leisering and R. Walker (eds) *The dynamics of modern society*, Bristol, Policy Press, 49–59.

Entwisle, D., Alexander, K. and Olson, L. (2002) 'Baltimore beginning school study in perspective', in E. Phelps, F. Frankenberg and A. Colby (eds) *Looking at lives: American longitudinal studies of the twentieth century*, New York, Russell Sage Foundation, 167–93.

ESRC (2016) *Framework for research ethics*. Online, available at: http://www.esrc.ac.uk/about-esrc/information/research-ethics.aspx [accessed 2016].

Fabian, J. (1983) *Time and the other: How anthropology makes its object*, Columbia, Columbia University Press.

Falola, B. (2015) 'Life geo-histories: Examining formative experiences and geographies', in N. Worth and I. Hardill (eds) *Researching the life course: Critical perspectives from the social sciences*, Bristol, Policy Press, 101–22.

Farrall, S., Hunter, B., Sharpe, G. and Calverley, A. (2014) *Criminal careers in transition*, Oxford, Oxford University Press.

Farrall, S., Hunter, B., Sharpe, G. and Calverley, A. (2016) 'What "works" when re-tracing sample members in a qualitative longitudinal study?' *International Journal of Social Research Methodology*, 19, 3, 287–300.

Farrell, C., Nice, K., Lewis, J. and Sainsbury, R. (2006) *Experiences of the 'Job Retention and Rehabilitation Pilot'*, Department for Work and Pensions, Research Report no. 339, Leeds, Corporate Document Service.

Filer, A. with Pollard, A. (1998) 'Developing the "Identity and Learning Programme": Principles and pragmatism in a longitudinal ethnography of pupil careers', in G. Walford (ed.) *Doing research about education*, London, Falmer Press, 57–75.

Filer, A. and Pollard, A. (2000) *The social world of pupil assessment: Processes and contexts of primary schooling*, London, Continuum.

Fincher, S. (2013) 'The diarist's audience', in L. Stanley (ed.) *Documents of life revisited*, London, Routledge, 77–91.

Firth, R. (1959) *Social change in Tikopia: Re-study of a Polynesian community after a generation*, London, George Allen and Unwin.

Flaherty, M. (2011) *The textures of time: Agency and temporal experience*, Philadelphia, Temple University Press.

Flowerdew, J. and Neale, B. (2003) 'Trying to stay apace: Children with multiple challenges in their post-divorce family lives', *Childhood*, 10, 2, 147–61.

Foster, G. (1979) 'Fieldwork in Tzintzuntzan: The first thirty years', in G. Foster, T. Scudder, E. Colson and R. Kemper (eds) *Long-term field research in social anthropology*, New York, Academic Press, 165–84.

Foster, G. (2002) 'A half-century of field research in Tzintzuntzan, Mexico: A personal view', in R. Kemper and A. Peterson Royce (eds) *Chronicling cultures: Long-term field research in anthropology*, Walnut Creek, Altamira Press, 252–83.

Foster, G., Scudder, T, Colson, E. and Kemper, R. (1979) (eds) *Long-term field research in social anthropology*, New York, Academic Press.

Freeman, M. (2010) *Hindsight: The promise and peril of looking backward*, Oxford, Oxford University Press.

Frith, H. (2011) 'Narrating biographical disruption and repair: Exploring the place of absent images in women's experiences of cancer and chemotherapy', in P. Reavey (ed.) *Visual methods in psychology*, London, Routledge, 55–68.

Furstenberg, F., Brooks-Gunn, J. and Morgan, S. (1987) *Adolescent mothers in later life*, Cambridge, Cambridge University Press.

Gale, N., Heath, G., Cameron, E., Rashid, S. and Redwood, S. (2013) 'Using the framework method for the analysis of qualitative data in multi-disciplinary health research', *BMC Medical Research Methodology*, 13, 117, 1–8.

Geertz, C. (1973) 'Thick description: Towards an interpretive theory of culture', in C. Geertz (ed.) *The interpretation of cultures: Selected essays*, New York, Basic Books, Chapter One.

George, L. (2009) 'Conceptualising and measuring trajectories', in G. Elder and J. Giele (eds) *The craft of life course research*, New York, Guilford Press, 163–86.

Gergen, K. (1973) 'Social psychology as history', *Journal of Personality and Social Psychology*, 26, 2, 309–20.

Gershuny, J. (2000) *Changing times: Work and leisure in post-industrial society*, Oxford, Oxford University Press.

Giddens, A. (1991) *Modernity and self identity: Self and society in the late modern age*, Cambridge, Polity.

Giele, J. (2009) 'Life stories to understand diversity: Variations by class, race and gender', in G. Elder and J. Giele (eds) *The craft of life course research*, New York, Guilford Press, 236–57.

Giele, J. and Elder, G. (1998) (eds) *Methods of life course research: Qualitative and quantitative approaches*, London, Sage.

Glaser, B. and Strauss, A. (1971) *Status passage*, Chicago, Aldine.

Goodwin, J. and O'Connor, H. (2015) 'A restudy of young workers from the 1960s: Researching intersections of work and life course in one locality over 50 years', in N. Worth and I. Hardill (eds) *Researching the life course: Critical perspectives from the social sciences*, Bristol, Policy Press, 63–80.

Gordon, T., Holland, J., Lahelma, E. and Thomson, R. (2005) 'Imagining gendered adulthood: Anxiety, ambivalence, avoidance and anticipation', *European Journal of Women's Studies*, 12, 1, 83–103.

Gordon, T. and Lahelma, E. (2003) 'From ethnography to life history: Tracing transitions of school children', *International Journal of Social Research Methodology*, 6, 3, 245–54.

Grandia, L. (2015) 'Slow ethnography: A hut with a view', *Critique of Anthropology*, 35, 3, 301–17.

Grbich, C. (2007) *Qualitative data analysis*, London, Sage.

Grenier, A. (2012) *Transitions and the life course: Challenging the constructions of growing older*, Bristol, Policy Press.

Grinyer, A. (2009) 'The anonymity of research participants: Assumptions, ethics and practicalities', *Pan*, 12, 49–58.

Grossoehme, D. and Lipstein, E. (2016) 'Analysing longitudinal qualitative data: The application of trajectory and recurrent cross-sectional approaches', *BMC Research Notes*, 9, 136.

Guenette, F. and Marshall, A. (2009) 'Time line drawings: Enhancing participant voice in narrative interviews on sensitive topics,' *International Journal of Qualitative Methods*, 8, 1, 86–92.

Guillemin, M. and Gillam, L. (2004) 'Ethics, reflexivity and "ethically important moments" in research', *Qualitative Inquiry*, 10, 2, 261–80.

Hackstaff, K., Kupferberg, F. and Negroni, C. (eds) (2012) *Biography and turning points in Europe and America*, Bristol, Policy Press.

Hagan, J. and McCarthy, B. (1997) *Mean streets*, Cambridge, Cambridge University Press.

Halbwachs, M. (1992) *On collective memory*, Chicago, Chicago University Press.

Hallden, G. (1994) 'Establishing order: Small girls write about family life', *Gender and Education*, 6, 1, 3–18.

Hallden, G. (1999) '"To be or not to be?": Absurd and humoristic descriptions as a strategy to avoid idyllic life stories: Boys write about family life', *Gender and Generation*, 11, 4, 469–79.

Hammersley, M. and Atkinson, P. (1995) *Ethnography: Principles in practice*, 2nd edn., London, Routledge.

Hammersley, M. and Traianou, A. (2012) *Ethics in qualitative research: Controversies and contexts*, London, Sage.

Hanna, E. and Lau-Clayton, C. (2012) *Capturing past and future time in QL field enquiry: Timelines and relational maps*, Timescapes Methods Guide series, no. 5, www.timescapes.leeds.ac.uk.

Harocopos, A. and Dennis, D. (2003) 'Maintaining contact with drug users over an 18 month period', *International Journal of Social Research Methodology*, 6, 3, 261–5.

Harden, J., Backett-Milburn, K., Hill, M. and MacLean, A. (2010) 'Oh, what a tangled web we weave: Experiences of doing "multiple perspectives" research in families', *International Journal of Social Research Methodology*, 13, 5, 441–52.

Harden, J., Maclean, A., Backett-Milburn, K. and Cunningham-Burley, S. (2012) 'The "family-work project": Children's and parents' experience of working parenthood' *Families, Relationships and Societies*, 1, 2, 207–22.

Hardgrove, A., Rootham, E. and McDowell, L. (2015) 'Possible selves in a precarious labour market: Youth, imagined futures and transitions to work in the UK', *Geoforum*, 60, 163–71.

Hareven, T. (1982) *Family time and industrial time: The relationship between family and work in a New England industrial community*, New York, Cambridge University Press.

Hareven, T. (2000) (ed.) *Families, history and social change: Life course and cross cultural perspectives*, Oxford, Westview Press.

Hareven, T. and Masaoka, K. (1988) 'Turning points and transitions: Perceptions of the life course', *Journal of Family History*, 13, 271–89.

Harris, C. (1987) 'The individual and society: A processual view', in A. Bryman, W. Bytheway, P. Allatt and T. Keil (eds) *Rethinking the life cycle*, Basingstoke, Macmillan, 17–29.

Heinz, W. (2003) 'Combining methods in life course research: A mixed blessing?' in W. Heinz and V. Marshall (eds) *Social dynamics of the life course*, New York, De Gruyter, 73–90.

Heinz, W. (2009) 'Transitions: Biography and agency', in W. Heinz, J. Huinink and A. Weymann (eds) *The life course reader: Individuals and societies across time*, Frankfurt, Campus Verlag, 421–9.

Heinz, W., Huinink, J. and Weymann, A. (2009) (eds) *The life course reader: Individuals and societies across time*, Frankfurt, Campus Verlag.

Hemmerman, L. (2010) 'Researching the hard to reach and the hard to keep: Notes from the field on longitudinal sample maintenance', in F. Shirani and S. Weller (eds) *Conducting qualitative longitudinal research: Fieldwork experiences*, Timescapes Working Paper Series no. 2 www.timescapes.leeds.ac.uk.

Henderson, S., Holland, J., McGrellis, S., Sharpe, S. and Thomson, R. (2007) *Inventing adulthoods: A biographical approach to youth transitions*, London, Sage.

Henderson, S., Holland, J., McGrellis, S., Sharpe, S. and Thomson, R. (2012) 'Storying qualitative longitudinal research: Sequence, voice and motif', *Qualitative Research*, 12, 1, 16–34.

Henwood, K. and Shirani, F. (2012) *Extending temporal horizons*, Timescapes Methods Guides Series no. 4, www.timescapes.leeds.ac.uk.

Henwood, K., Shirani, F. and Finn, M. (2011) '"So you think you've moved, changed, the representation got more what?" Methodological and analytical reflections on visual (photo-elicitation) methods used in the "Men as Fathers' study"', in P. Reavey (ed.) *Visual methods in psychology*, London, Routledge, 330–45.

Hermanowicz, J. (2016) 'Longitudinal qualitative research', in M. Shanahan, J. Mortimer, and M. Johnson (eds) *Handbook of the life course, Volume 11*, New York, Springer, 491–513.

Hockey, J. and James, A. (2003) *Social Identities across the life course*, Basingstoke, Palgrave Macmillan.

Holland, J. and Edwards, R. (2014) (eds) *Understanding families over time: Research and policy*, London, Palgrave Macmillan.

Holland, J. and Thomson, R. (2009) 'Gaining a perspective on choice and fate: Revisiting critical moments', *European Societies*, 11, 3, 451–69.

Holland, J., Thomson, R. and Henderson, S. (2006) *Qualitative longitudinal research: A discussion paper*, Working Paper no. 21, London South Bank University.

Holmberg, D. (2012) 'Contingency, collaboration and the unimagined over thirty-five years of ethnography', in S. Howell and A. Talle (eds) *Returns to the field: Multi-temporal research and contemporary anthropology*, Bloomington, Indiana University Press, 95–122.

Holstein, J. and Gubrium, J. (2000) *Constructing the life course*, 2nd edn, New York, General Hall.

Howell, S. (2012) 'Cumulative understandings: Experiences from the study of two Southeast Asian societies', in S. Howell, and A. Talle (eds) *Returns to the field: Multi-temporal research and contemporary anthropology*, Bloomington, Indiana University Press, 153–79.

Howell, S. and Talle, A. (2012) (eds) *Returns to the field: Multi-temporal research and contemporary anthropology*, Bloomington, Indiana University Press.

Huber, G. and Van de Ven, A. (1995) (eds) *Longitudinal field research methods: Studying processes of organisational change*, London, Sage.

Hughes, K. (2011) *Ethics in qualitative longitudinal research: A special case?* Presentation for the Timescapes QL methods training programme, University of Leeds, October.

Iantaffi, A. (2011) 'Travelling along rivers of experience: Personal construct theory and visual metaphors in research', in P. Reavey (ed.) *Visual methods in psychology*, London, Routledge, 271–83.

Irwin, S. (2013) 'Qualitative secondary analysis in practice: Introduction', *Families, Relationships and Societies*, 2, 2, 285–8. [Open Space on QSA]

Irwin, S., Bornat, J. and Winterton, M. (2012) 'Timescapes secondary analysis: Comparison, context and working across datasets', *Qualitative Research*, 12, 1, 66–80.

Irwin, S. and Winterton, M. (2014) 'Gender and work-family conflict: A secondary analysis of "Timescapes" data', in J. Holland and R. Edwards (eds) *Understanding families over time: Research and policy*, London, Palgrave Macmillan, 142–60.

Johnson, D. (2015) 'Not your stereotypical young father, not your typical teenage life', *Families, Relationships and Societies*, 4, 2, 319–22. [Open space on young fatherhood].

Jost, G. (2012) 'Biographical structuring through a critical life event: Parental loss during childhood', in K. Hackstaff, F. Kupferberg, and C. Negroni (eds) *Biography and turning points in Europe and America*, Bristol, Policy Press, 125–42.

Kelly, A. (2008) 'Living loss: An exploration of the internal space of liminality', *Mortality*, 13, 4, 335–50.

Kelly, J. and McGrath, J. (1988) *On time and method*, London, Sage.

Kemper, R. and Peterson Royce, A. (2002) (eds) *Chronicling cultures: Long term field research in anthropology*, Walnut Creek, Altamira Press.

King, H. and Roberts, B. (2015) 'Biographical research, longitudinal study and theorisation', in M. O'Neill, B. Roberts and A. Sparkes (eds) *Advances in biographical methods: Creative applications*, London, Routledge, 106–22.

Kohli, M. (1981) 'Biography: Account, text, method', in D. Bertaux (ed.) *Biography and society*, London, Sage, 61–75.

Krings, T., Moriarty, E., Wickham, J., Bobek, A. and Salamonska, J. (2013) *New mobilities in Europe: Polish migration to Ireland post 2004*, Manchester, Manchester University Press.

Kupferberg, F. (2012) 'Conclusion: Theorising turning points and decoding narratives', in K. Hackstaff, F. Kupferberg and C. Negroni (eds) *Biography and turning points in Europe and America*, Bristol, Policy Press, 227–59.

Land, E. and Patrick, R. (2014) *The process of using participatory research methods with film-making to disseminate research: Challenges and potential*, SAGE Research Methods Cases, London, Sage. [Report on the development of the Dole Animators Film (2015) *All in this together? Are benefits ever a life style choice?* www.doleanimators.org.].

Lassiter, L. (2012) '"To fill in the missing piece of the Middletown puzzle": Lessons from re-studying Middletown', *The Sociological Review*, 60, 3, 421–37.

Laub, J. and Sampson, R. (1998) 'Integrating quantitative and qualitative data', in J. Giele and G. Elder (eds) *Methods of life course research: Qualitative and quantitative approaches*, London, Sage, 213–30.

Laub, J. and Sampson, R. (2003) *Shared beginnings, divergent lives: Delinquent boys to age 70*, Cambridge, MA, Harvard University Press.

Lee, J. (2015) 'Using a life history approach within transnational ethnography: A case study of Korean New Zealander returnees', in N. Worth and I. Hardill (eds) *Researching the life course: Critical perspectives from the social sciences*, Bristol, Policy Press, 183–98.

Leisering, L. and Walker, R. (1998) (eds) *The dynamics of modern society*, Bristol, Policy Press.

Lemke, J. (2000) 'Across the scales of time: Artifacts, activities and meanings in ecosocial systems', *Mind, Culture and Activity*, 7, 4, 273–90.

Leonard-Barton, D. (1995) 'A dual methodology for case studies', in G. Huber and A. Van de Ven (eds) *Longitudinal field research methods: Studying processes of organisational change*, London, Sage, 38–64.

Levi-Strauss, C. (1966) *The savage mind*, Chicago, Chicago University Press.

Lewis, J. (2007) 'Analysing qualitative longitudinal research in evaluations', *Social Policy and Society*, 6, 4, 545–56.

Lewis, O. (1951) *Life in a Mexican village: Tepoztlan restudied*, Urbana, University of Illinois Press.

Lewthwaite, S. and Bartlett, R. (2017) 'Diary methods: Voyages into the interior', *MethodsNews*, 2017, 2, 2.

Lindsey, R., Metcalfe, E. and Edwards, R. (2015) 'Time in mixed methods longitudinal research: Working across written narratives and large scale panel survey data to investigate attitudes to volunteering', in N. Worth and I. Hardill (eds) *Researching the life course: Critical perspectives from the social sciences*, Bristol, Policy Press, 43–62.

Lopez-Aguado, P. (2012) 'Working between two worlds: Gang intervention and street liminality', *Ethnography*, 14, 2, 186–206.

Loumidis, A., Stafford, B., Youngs, R., Green, A., Arthur, S., Legard, R. *et al.* (2001) *Evaluation of the 'New deal for disabled people personal adviser service pilot': Final report*, DSS Research Reports: 144, Leeds, Corporate Document Services.

Lovgren, M, Hamberg, K. and Tishelman, C. (2010) 'Clock time and embodied time experienced by patients with operable lung cancer', *Cancer Nursing*, 33, 1, 55–63.

Lynd, R. and Lynd, H. (1929) *Middletown: A study in contemporary American culture*, New York, Harcourt Brace.

Lynd, R. and Lynd, H. (1937) *Middletown in transition: A study in cultural conflicts*, New York, Harcourt Brace.

Lyon, D. and Crow, G. (2012) 'The challenges and opportunities of re-studying community on the Isle of Sheppey: Young people's imagined futures', *The Sociological Review*, 60, 3, 498–517.

MacLean, A. and Harden, J. (2012) *Generating group accounts with parents and children in qualitative longitudinal research: A practical and ethical guide*, Timescapes Methods Guide Series no. 8, www.timescapes. leeds.ac.uk.

Macmillan, R., Arvidson, A., Edwards, S., Soteri-Proctor, A., Taylor, R. and Teasdale, S. (2011) *First impressions: Introducing the 'Real Times' third sector case studies*, Third Sector Research Centre Working Paper 67, Birmingham, TSRC.

Macmillan, R., Arvidson, A., Edwards, S., Soteri-Proctor, A., Taylor, R. and Teasdale, S. (2012) *What happens next? Researching the Third Sector using qualitative longitudinal methods*, Timescapes Methods Guides Series no. 15, www.timescapes.leeds.ac.uk.

Mannay, D. (2015) *Visual, narrative and creative research methods*, London, Routledge.

Mannheim, K. (1952[1927]) 'The problem of generations', in P. Kecskemeti (ed.) *Essays on the sociology of knowledge: The collected works of Karl Mannheim, Vol 5*, London, Routledge, 276–322.

Mauthner, N. and Parry, O. (2013) 'Open access digital data sharing: Principles, policies and practices', *Social Epistemology*, 27, 1, 47–67.

May, J. and Thrift, N. (eds) (2001) *Timespace: Geographies of temporality*, New York, Routledge.

McDonald, P., Pini, B., Bailey, J. and Price, R. (2011) 'Young people's aspirations for education, work, family and leisure', *Work, Employment and Society*, 25, 1, 68–84.

McLeod, J. (2003) 'Why we interview now: Reflexivity and perspective in a longitudinal study', *International Journal of Social Research Methodology*, 6, 3, 201–11.

142    *References*

McLeod, J. and Thomson, R. (2009) *Researching social change*, London, Sage.

McNaughton, C. (2008) *Crossing the continuum: Understanding routes out of homelessness, and examining 'what works'*, Glasgow, Simon Community Project.

Merrill, B. and West, L. (2009) *Using biographical methods in social research*, London, Sage.

Midgley, M. (2014) *Are you an illusion?* London, Routledge.

Millar, J. (2007) (ed.) 'Qualitative longitudinal research for social policy', *Social Policy and Society*, 6, 4, 529–94.

Miller, R. (2000) *Researching life stories and family histories*, London, Sage.

Miller, T. (2005) *Making sense of motherhood: A narrative approach*, Cambridge, Cambridge University Press.

Miller, T. (2015) 'Going back: Stalking, talking and research responsibilities in qualitative longitudinal research', *International Journal of Social Research Methodology*, 18, 3, 293–305.

Miller, T. (2017) *Making sense of parenthood: Caring, gender and family lives*, Cambridge, Cambridge University Press.

Miller, T. and Bell, L. (2002) 'Consenting to what? Issues of access, gate-keeping and informed consent', in M. Mauthner, M. Birch, J. Jessop and T. Miller (eds) *Ethics in qualitative research*, London, Sage, 53–69.

Mills, C. W. (1959) *The sociological imagination*, Oxford, Oxford University Press.

Mitchell, C., De Lange, N. and Moletsane, R. (2017) (eds) *Participatory visual methodologies: Social change, community and policy*, London, Sage.

Molloy, D. and Woodfield, K. with Bacon, J. (2002) *Longitudinal qualitative research approaches in evaluation studies*, Department for Work and Pensions Working Paper no. 7, London, HMSO.

Monrouxe, L. (2009) 'Solicited audio diaries in longitudinal narrative research: A view from inside', *Qualitative Research*, 9, 1, 81–103.

Moore, N. (2007) '(Re) using qualitative data', *Sociological Research Online*, 12, 3, 1.

Moore, N. (2012) 'The politics and ethics of naming: Questioning anonymization in (archival) research', *International Journal of Social Research Methodology*, 15, 4, 331–40.

Morrow, V. (2009) *The ethics of social research with children and families in 'Young Lives': Practical experiences*, Young Lives Working Paper

Series no 53, Department of International Development, University of Oxford.

Morrow, V. (2013) 'Practical ethics in social research with children and families in "Young Lives": A longitudinal study of childhood poverty in Ethiopia, Andhra Pradesh (India), Peru and Vietnam', *Methodological Innovations Online*, 8, 2, 21–35.

Morrow, V. and Crivello, G. (2015) 'What is the value of qualitative longitudinal research with children and young people for international development?' *International Journal of Social Research Methodology*, 18, 3, 267–80.

Neale, B. (2012) *Qualitative longitudinal research: An introduction to the 'Timescape's methods guides series*, Methods Guide no. 1, www.timescapes.leeds.ac.uk.

Neale, B. (2013) 'Adding time into the mix: Stakeholder ethics in qualitative longitudinal research', *Methodological Innovations Online*, 8, 2, 6–20.

Neale, B. (2015) 'Time and the life course: Perspectives from qualitative longitudinal research', in N. Worth and I. Hardill (eds) *Researching the life course: Critical perspectives from the social sciences*, Bristol, Policy Press, 25–41.

Neale, B. (2016) 'Introduction: Young fatherhood: Lived experiences and policy challenges,' *Social Policy and Society*, 15, 1, 75–83. [Themed section on young fatherhood].

Neale, B. (2017a) *Generating data in qualitative longitudinal research: A review of field tools and techniques*, Timescapes Working Paper no. 8, www.timescapes.leeds.ac.uk.

Neale, B. (2017b) *Research data as documents of life*, Guest-Post no. 13, www.bigqlr.ncrm.ac.uk.

Neale, B. and Bishop, L. (2012) 'The "Timescapes Archive": A stakeholder approach to archiving qualitative longitudinal data', *Qualitative Research*, 12, 1, 53–65.

Neale, B. and Davies, L. (2016) 'Becoming a young breadwinner? The education, employment and training trajectories of young fathers', *Social Policy and Society*, 15,1, 85–98.

Neale, B. and Flowerdew, J. (2003) 'Time, textures and childhood: The contours of longitudinal qualitative research', *International Journal of Social Research Methodology*, 6, 3, 189–99.

Neale, B. and Flowerdew, J. (2004) *Parent problems! Looking back at our parents' divorce*, East Molesey, Surrey, Young Voice.

Neale, B. and Flowerdew, J. (2007) 'New structures, new agency: The dynamics of child-parent relationships after divorce', *International Journal of Children's Rights*, 15, 1, 25–42.

Neale, B., Henwood, K. and Holland, J. (2012) (eds) 'Researching lives through time: The "Timescapes" approach', *Qualitative Research*, 12, 1, 1–15. [Special issue on Timescapes]

Neale, B., Lau-Clayton, C., Davies, L. and Ladlow, L. (2015) *Researching the lives of young fathers: The 'Following Young Fathers' study and dataset*, Briefing Paper no. 8, www. followingfathers.leeds.ac.uk/ findingsandpublications.

Neale, B. and Morton, S. (2012) *Creating impact through qualitative longitudinal research*, Timescapes Methods Guides Series no. 20, www.timescapes.leeds.ac.uk.

Neale, B., Proudfoot, R., Blyth, G., Hughes, K., and Phillips, B. (2016) *Managing qualitative longitudinal data: A practical guide*, www. timescapesarchive.ac.uk.

Negroni, C. (2012) 'Turning points in the life course: A narrative concept in professional bifurcations', in K. Hackstaff, F. Kupferberg and C. Negroni (eds) *Biography and turning Points in Europe and America*, Bristol, Policy Press, 41–64.

Neumann, I. (2012) 'Introduction to the forum on liminality', *Review of International Studies*, 38, 473–9 [special issue on liminality].

Nielsen, H. B. (2003) 'Historical, cultural and emotional meanings: Interviews with young girls in three generations,' *NORA (Nordic Journal of women's studies)* 11, 1, 14–26.

Nowotny, H. (1994) *Time: The modern and postmodern experience*, Cambridge, Polity Press.

O'Connor, H. and Goodwin, J. (2010) 'Utilising data from a lost sociological project: Experiences, insights, promises', *Qualitative Research*, 10, 3, 283–98.

O'Connor, H. and Goodwin, J. (2012) 'Revisiting Norbert Elias's sociology of community: Learning from the Leicester re-studies', *The Sociological Review*, 60, 476–97.

O'Connor, P. (2006) 'Young people's construction of the self: Late modern elements and gender differences', *Sociology*, 40, 1, 107–24.

O'Neill, M., Roberts, B. and Sparkes, A. (2015) (eds) *Advances in biographical methods: Creative applications*, London, Routledge.

O'Reilly, K. (2012) 'Ethnographic returning, qualitative longitudinal research and the reflexive analysis of social practice', *The Sociological Review*, 60, 518–36.

Ottenberg, S. (1990) 'Thirty years of field notes: Changing relationships to the text', in R. Sanjek (ed.) *Fieldnotes: The making of anthropology*, Ithaca, Cornell University Press.

Pahl, R. (1978) 'Living without a job: How school leavers see the future', *New Society*, 2nd November, 259–62.

Parkinson, S., Eatough, V., Holmes, J., Stapley, E. and Midgley, N. (2016) 'Framework analysis: A worked example of a study exploring young people's experiences of depression', *Qualitative Research in Psychology*, 13, 2, 109–29.

Patrick, R. (2012) *Recruiting and sustaining population samples over time*, Timescapes Methods Guide Series no. 3, www.timescapes.leeds.ac.uk.

Patrick, R. (2017) *For whose benefit? The everyday realities of welfare reform*, Bristol, Policy Press.

Patterson, L., Forbes, K. and Peace, R. (2009) 'Happy, stable and contented: Accomplished ageing in the imagined futures of young New Zealanders', *Ageing and Society*, 29, 431–54

Pawson, R. (2006) *Evidence-based policy: A realist perspective*, London, Sage.

Pearson, H. (2016) *The life project*, London, Allen Lane.

Pember Reeves, M. (2008 [1913]) *Round about a pound a week*, London, Persephone Books.

Perks, R. and Thomson, A. (2016) (eds) *The oral history reader*, 3rd edn., London, Routledge.

Peterson Royce, A. (2005) 'The long and short of it: Benefits and challenges of long-term ethnographic research', Paper presented at the ESRC seminar series: *Qualitative longitudinal research: Principles, practice, policy*, University of Leeds, September 30th.

Peterson Royce, A. and Kemper, R. (2002) 'Long-term field research: metaphors, paradigms and themes', in R. Kemper and A. Peterson Royce (eds) *Chronicling cultures: Long-term field research in anthropology*, Walnut Creek, Altamira Press, xiii–xxxviii.

Pettigrew, A. (1995) 'Longitudinal field research on change: Theory and practice', in G. Huber, and A. Van de Ven (eds) *Longitudinal field research methods*, London, Sage, 91–125.

Phelps, E., Furstenberg, F. and Colby, A. (2002) (eds) *Looking at lives: American longitudinal studies of the twentieth century*, New York, Russell Sage Foundation.

Philip, G (2017) *Working with qualitative longitudinal data*, Guest Blog, http://bigqlr.ncrm.ac.uk.

Pilcher, J. (1994) 'Mannheim's sociology of generations: An undervalued legacy', *British Journal of Sociology*, 45, 3, 481–95.

Pini, M. and Walkerdine, V. (2011) 'Girls on film: Video diaries as auto-ethnography', in P. Reavey (ed.) *Visual methods in psychology*, London, Routledge, 139–52.

Plummer, K. (2001) *Documents of Life 2: An invitation to a critical humanism*, London, Sage.

Plumridge, L. and Thomson, R. (2003) 'Longitudinal qualitative studies and the reflexive self', *International Journal of Social Research Methodology*, 6, 3, 213–22.

Pollard, A. (2007) 'The Identity and Learning Programme: "Principled pragmatism" in a 12-year longitudinal ethnography', *Ethnography and Education*, 2, 1, 1–19.

Pollard, A. with Filer, A. (1996) *The social world of children's learning: Case studies of pupils from four to seven*, London, Cassell.

Pollard, A. and Filer, A. (1999) *The social world of pupil career: Strategic biographies through primary school*, London, Cassell.

Portelli, A. (2016 [1979]) 'What makes oral history different?' in R. Perks, and A. Thomson (eds) *The oral history reader*, 3rd edn., London, Routledge, 48–58.

Rapley, T. (2016) 'Some pragmatics of qualitative data analysis', in D. Silverman (ed.) *Qualitative research*, 4th edn., London, Sage.

Reiss, M. (2005) 'Managing endings in a longitudinal study: Respect for persons', *Research in Science Education*, 35, 123–35.

Reiter, H., Rogge, B. and Schoneck, N. (2011) 'Times of life in times of change: Sociological perspectives on time and the life course', *BIOS*, 24, 2, 171–4.

Riessman, C. (2008) 'Concluding comments', in M. Andrews, C. Squire, and M. Tamboukou (eds) *Doing narrative research*, London, Sage, 151–6.

Riley, M. (1998) 'A life course approach: Autobiographical notes', in J. Giele and G. Elder (eds) *Methods of life course research: Qualitative and quantitative approaches*, London, Sage, 28–51.

Ritchie, J. and Lewis. J. (2003) (eds) *Qualitative research practice*, London, Sage.

Ritchie, J., Lewis, J., McNaughton Nicholls, C. and Ormston, R. (2014) (eds) *Qualitative research practice*, London, Sage, 2nd edn.

Robards, B. and Lincoln, S. (2017) 'Uncovering longitudinal life narratives: Scrolling back on Facebook', *Qualitative Research*, 17, 6, 715–30.

Roberts, B. (2002) *Biographical research*, Buckingham, Open University Press.

Rosa, H. (2013) *Social acceleration: A new theory of modernity*, New York, Columbia University Press.

Rosser, C. and Harris, C. (1965) *The family and social change*, London, Routledge and Kegan Paul.

Rothman, K., Gallacher, J. and Hatch, E. (2013) 'Why representativeness should be avoided', *International Journal of Epidemiology*, 42, 1012–4.

Ruspini, E. (2002) *Introduction to longitudinal research*, London, Routledge.

Saldana, J. (2003) *Longitudinal qualitative research: Analyzing change through time*, Walnut Creek, Altamira Press.

Sanders, J. and Munford, R. (2008) 'Losing sense to the future? Young women's strategic responses to adulthood transitions', *Journal of Youth Studies*, 11, 3, 331–46.

Scheper-Hughes, N. (2000) 'Ire in Ireland', *Ethnography*, 1, 1, 117–40.

Schmidt-Thome, K. (2015) 'Triangulation with softGIS in life course research: Situated action possibilities and embodied knowledge', in N. Worth and I. Hardill (eds) *Researching the life course: Critical perspectives from the social sciences*, Bristol, Policy Press, 161–82.

Scott, J. and Alwin, D. (1998) 'Retrospective versus prospective measurement of life histories in longitudinal research', in J. Giele and G. Elder (eds) *Methods of life course research: Qualitative and quantitative approaches*, London, Sage, 98–127.

Scudder, T. and Colson, E. (2002) 'Long-term research in Gwembe Valley, Zambia', in R. Kemper. and A. Peterson Royce (eds) *Chronicling cultures: Long-term field research in anthropology*, Walnut Creek, Altamira Press, 197–238.

Shah, S. and Priestley, M. (2011) *Disability and social change: Private lives and public policy*, Bristol, Policy Press.

Shanahan, M. and Macmillan, R. (2008) *Biography and the sociological imagination: Contexts and contingencies*, New York, Norton.

Shaw, C. (1966 [1930]) *The Jack Roller: A delinquent boy's own story*, Chicago, University of Chicago Press.

Shaw, J. (2001) 'Winning territory: Changing place to change pace', in J. May and N. Thrift (eds) *Timespace: Geographies of temporality*, New York, Routledge, 120–32.

Shirani, F. and Henwood, K. (2011) 'Taking each day as it comes: Temporal experiences in the context of unexpected life course transitions', *Time and Society*, 20, 1, 49–68.

Smith, N. (2003) 'Cross-sectional profiling and longitudinal analysis: Research notes on analysis in the LQ study "Negotiating transitions in Citizenship"', *International Journal of Social Research Methodology*, 6, 3, 273–7.

Srivastava, P. and Hopwood, N. (2009) 'A practical iterative framework for qualitative data analysis', *International Journal of Qualitative Methods*, 8, 1, 76–84.

Stacey, M. (1960) *Tradition and change: A study of Banbury*, Oxford, Oxford University Press.

Stacey, M., Batstone, E., Bell, C, and Murcott, A. (1975) *Power, persistence and change*, London, Routledge and Kegan Paul.

Stanley, L. (2013) 'Whites writing: Letters and documents of life in a QLR project', in L. Stanley (ed.) *Documents of life revisited: Narrative and biographical methodology for a 21st century critical humanism*, London, Routledge, 59–73.

Stanley, L. (2015) 'Operationalising a QLR project on social change and whiteness in South Africa, 1770s - 1970s', *International Journal of Social Research Methodology*, 18, 3, 251–65.

Strauss, A. (1997 [1959]) *Mirrors and masks: The search for identity*, New Brunswick, Transaction Publishers.

Swallow, V., Newton, J. and Van Lottum, C. (2003) 'How to manage and display qualitative data using Framework and Microsoft Excel', *Journal of Clinical Nursing*, 12, 610–2.

Szakolczai, A. (2014) 'Living permanent liminality: The recent transition experience in Ireland', *Irish Journal of Sociology*, 22, 1, 28–50.

Talle, A. (2012) 'Returns to the Maasai: Multi-temporal fieldwork and the production of anthropological knowledge', in S. Howell and A. Talle (eds) *Returns to the field: Multi-temporal research and contemporary anthropology*, Bloomington, Indiana University Press, 73–94.

Tarrant, A. and Neale, B. (2017) (eds) *Learning to support young dads: Responding to young fathers in a different way*, Policy Briefing, Supporting Young Dads Impact Initiative, www.followingfathers.leeds. ac.uk/impact.

Taylor, R. (2015) 'Beyond anonymity: Temporality and the production of knowledge in a qualitative longitudinal study', *International Journal of Social Research Methodology*, 18, 3, 281–92

Thomas, W. I. and Znaniecki, F. (1958 [1918-21]) *The Polish peasant in Europe and America*, New York, Dover Publications.

Thompson, P. (1981) 'Life histories and the analysis of social change', in D. Bertaux (ed.) *Biography and society: The life history approach in the social sciences*, London, Sage, 289–306.

Thompson, P. (2000) *The voice of the past*, 3rd edn., Oxford, Oxford University Press.

Thomson, R. (2007) 'The qualitative longitudinal case history: Practical, methodological and ethical reflections', *Social Policy and Society*, 6, 4, 571–82.

Thomson, R. (2009) *Unfolding lives: Youth, gender and change*, Bristol, Policy Press.

Thomson, R. (2010a) (ed.) *Intensity and insight: Qualitative longitudinal methods as a route to the psycho-social*, Timescapes Working paper no. 3, www.timescapes.leeds.ac.uk.

Thomson, R. (2010b) 'Creating family case histories: Subjects, selves and family dynamics', in R. Thomson (ed.) *Intensity and insight: Qualitative longitudinal methods as a route to the psycho-social*, Timescapes Working paper no. 3, 6–18, www.timescapes.leeds.ac.uk.

Thomson, R. (2011) 'Using biographical and longitudinal methods: Researching mothering', in J. Mason and A. Dale (eds) *Understanding social research*, London, Sage, 62–74.

Thomson, R. (2012) *Qualitative longitudinal methods as a route into the psycho-social*, Timescapes Methods Guides Series Guide no. 13, www.timescapes.ac.uk.

Thomson, R., Bell, R., Henderson, S., Holland, J., McGrellis, S. and Sharpe, S. (2002) 'Critical moments: Choice, chance and opportunity in young people's narratives of transition to adulthood', *Sociology* 36, 335–54.

Thomson, R. and Holland, J. (2002) 'Imagined adulthood: Resources, plans and contradictions', *Gender and Education*, 14, 4, 337–50.

Thomson, R. and Holland, J. (2003) 'Hindsight, foresight and insight: The challenges of longitudinal qualitative research', *International Journal of Social Research Methodology*, 6, 3, 233–44.

Thomson, R. and Holland, J. (2005) '"Thanks for the memory": Memory books as a methodological resource in biographical research', *Qualitative Research*, 5, 2, 201–19.

Thomson, R., Kehily, M., Hadfield, L. and Sharpe, S. (2011) *Making modern mothers*, Bristol, Policy Press.

Thomson, R. and McLeod, J. (2015) (eds) 'New frontiers in qualitative longitudinal research: An agenda for research', *International Journal of Social Research Methodology*, 18, 3, 243–50. [Special issue on qualitative longitudinal research].

Thomson, R., Plumridge, L. and Holland, J. (2003) (eds) 'Editorial: Longitudinal qualitative research: A developing methodology', *International Journal of Social Research Methodology*, 6, 3185–7. [Special issue on longitudinal qualitative research].

Van de Ven, A. and Huber, G. (1995) 'Introduction', in G. Huber and A. Van de Ven (eds) *Longitudinal field research methods: Studying processes of organisational change*, London, Sage, vii–xiv.

Van Gennep, A. (1960 [1909]) *The rites of passage*, London, Routledge and Kegan Paul.

Van Houte, M. (2017) *Return migration to Afghanistan*, London, Palgrave Macmillan.

Veness, T. (1962) *School leavers: Their aspirations and expectations*, London, Methuen.

Vogl, S., Zartler, U., Schmidt, E. and Rieder, I. (2017) 'Developing an analytical framework for multiple perspective, qualitative longitudinal interviews', *International Journal of Social Research Methodology*, published online 29th June.

Wajcman, J. (2015) *Pressed for time*, Chicago, Chicago University Press.

Walkerdine, V., Lucey, H. and Melody, J. (2001) *Growing up girl: Psycho-social explorations of gender and class*, London, Palgrave Macmillan.

Wallace, G., Ruddick, J., Flutter, J. with Harris, S. (1998) 'Using ethnographic methods in a study of students' secondary school and post–school careers', in G. Walford (ed.) *Doing research about education*, London, Falmer Press, 76–92.

Ward, J. and Henderson, Z. (2003) 'Some practical and ethical issues encountered while conducting tracking research with young people leaving the "care" system', *International Journal of Social Research Methodology*, 6, 3, 255–9.

Warin, J. (2010) *Stories of self: Tracking children's identity and wellbeing through the school years*, Stoke on Trent, Trentham.

Warin, J. (2011) 'Ethical mindfulness and reflexivity: Managing a research relationship with children and young people in a fourteen year qualitative longitudinal research (QLR) study', *Qualitative Inquiry*, 17, 10, 805–14.

Watson, C. (2013) 'Between diary and memoir: Documenting a life in war time Britain', in L. Stanley (ed.) *Documents of life revisited*, London, Routledge, 107–19.

Weller, S. (2012) 'Evolving creativity in qualitative longitudinal research with children and teenagers', *International Journal of Social Research Methodology*, 15, 2, 119–33.

Wengraf, T. (2000) 'Uncovering the general from within the particular: From contingencies to typologies in the understanding of cases', in P. Chamberlayne, J. Bornat and T. Wengraf (eds) *The turn to biographical methods in social science*, London, Routledge, 140–64.

Wiles, R. (2012) 'Developing ethical literacy: An unnecessary burden or a benefit to researchers?' *NCRM Methods News*, Winter, 7.

Wiles, R. (2013) *What are qualitative research ethics?* London, Bloomsbury Academic.

Williamson, E., Abrahams, H., Morgan, K. and Cameron, A. (2014) 'Tracking homeless women in qualitative longitudinal research', *European Journal of Homelessness*, 8, 2, 69–91.

Wilson, M. (1977) *For men and elders: Changes in the relations of generations and of men and women among the Nyakyusa-Ngonde people, 1875-1971*, London, International African Institute.

Wingens, M. and Reiter, H. (2011) 'The life course approach – It's about time!', *BIOS*, 24, 2, 87–203.

Winterton, M. and Irwin, S. (2011) 'Youngsters' expectations and context: Secondary analysis and interpretations of imagined futures', in M. Winterton, G. Crow and B. Morgan-Brett (eds) *Young lives and imagined futures: Insights from archived data,* Timescapes Working Paper no. 6, www.timescapes.leeds.ac.uk.

Winterton, M. and Irwin, S. (2012) 'Teenage expectations of going to university: The ebb and flow of influences from 14 to 18', *Journal of Youth Studies,* 15, 7, 858–74.

Wiseman, V., Conteh, L. and Matovu, F. (2005) 'Using diaries to collect data in resource-poor settings: Questions of design and implementation', *Health Policy and Planning,* 20, 6, 394–404.

Woodman, D and Wyn, J. (2013) 'Youth policy and generations: Why youth policy needs to "re-think youth"', *Social Policy and Society,* 12, 2, 265–75.

Worth, N. (2009) 'Understanding youth transitions as "becoming": Identity, time and futurity', *Geoforum,* 40, 1050–60.

Worth, N. (2011) 'Evaluating life maps as a versatile method for life course geographies', *Area,* 43, 4, 405–12.

Worth, N. and Hardill, I. (2015) (eds) *Researching the life course: Critical perspectives from the social sciences,* Bristol, Policy Press.

Yardley, A. (2008) 'Piecing together: A methodological bricolage', *Forum: Qualitative Social Research,* 9, 2, Art 31.

Zerubavel, E. (1979) *Patterns of time in hospital life: A sociological perspective,* Chicago, University of Chicago Press.

Zerubavel, E. (1981) *Hidden rhythms: Schedules and calendars in social life,* Chicago, University of Chicago Press.

Zerubavel, E. (2003) *Time maps: Collective memory and the social shape of the past,* Chicago, University of Chicago Press.

Zimmerman, D. and Wieder, D. (1977) 'The diary: Diary-interview method', *Urban Life,* 5, 4, 479–97.

# Index